Disaster Recovery Using VMware vSphere Replication and vCenter Site Recovery Manager

Learn to deploy and use vSphere Replication 5.5 as a standalone disaster recovery solution and to orchestrate disaster recovery using vCenter Site Recovery Manager 5.5

Abhilash GB

BIRMINGHAM - MUMBAI

Disaster Recovery Using VMware vSphere Replication and vCenter Site Recovery Manager

First Published: May 2014

Production reference: 1190514

Published by Packt Publishing Ltd.
Livery Place
35 Livery Street
Birmingham B3 2PB, UK.

ISBN 978-1-78217-644-2

www.packtpub.com

Cover Image by Gerard Eykhoff (gerard@eykhoff.nl)

Credits

About the Author

Abhilash GB is an author, a designer, and a VMware vExpert 2014, who specializes in the areas of Data Center Virtualization and cloud computing.

He is a VMware Certified Advanced Professional in Data Center Administration (VCAP4-DCA and VCAP5-DCA). He has been in the IT industry for nearly a decade, and he has been working on VMware products and technologies since the start of 2007. He is also the author of *VMware vSphere 5.1 Cookbook, Packt Publishing*.

He is a passionate author who's willing to contribute more titles to the VMware community, and also an aspiring engineer always ready to indulge in designing and creating great solutions for customers.

I would like to dedicate this book to my wife and my parents. Without their patience and support, this book would not have been possible.

Thanks to the technical reviewers Andy Grant, Kenneth van Ditmarsch, and Daniel Langenhan for their invaluable inputs.

Special thanks to Nikhil Chinnari (Acquisition Editor), Harshal Ved (Project Coordinator), Govindan K (Content Development Editor), and Shashank Desai and Menza Mathew (Technical Editors) for their support during the course of writing this book.

About the Reviewers

Kenneth van Ditmarsch is a highly experienced freelance virtualization consultant. Being one of the few VMware Certified Design Experts (VCDX), he has clearly added value in virtualization infrastructure projects. His knowledge and extensive project experience was gained especially during his last years at VMware and several specialized consulting firms.

Kenneth agreed on reviewing this book mainly because he is currently working on projects based on several VMware Site Recovery Managers. Kenneth has a personal blog on virtualization that can be accessed at `http://www.virtualkenneth.com`.

Andy Grant is a technical consultant for HP Enterprise Services. Andy's primary focus is Data Center infrastructure and virtualization projects across a number of industries, including government, healthcare, forestry, financial, gas and oil, and international contracting. He currently holds a number of technical certifications, including VCAP4/5-DCA/DCD, VCP4/5, MCITP: EA, MCSE, CCNA, Security+, A+, and ASE - HP BladeSystem.

Outside of work, Andy enjoys hiking, action pistol sports, and spending time adventuring with his son.

Daniel Langenhan is a client-focused virtualization expert with more than 18 years of international industry experience.

His skills span the breadth of virtualization ranging from architecture, design, and implementation for large multitier enterprise client systems to delivering captivating education and training sessions in security technologies and practices to diverse audiences.

Utilizing his extensive knowledge, experience, and skills, he has a proven track record of successful integration of virtualization into different business areas, while minimizing cost and maximizing reliability and effectiveness of the solution for his clients.

He gained experience from Australian, European, and international enterprise clients. Daniel's consulting company is well established, with strong industry ties in many verticals, such as finance, telecommunications, and print. His consulting business also provides services to VMware International Ltd.

He has authored the following books:

- *Instant VMware vCloud Starter*, *Packt Publishing*
- *VMware View Security Essentials*, *Packt Publishing*
- *VMware vCloud Director Cookbook*, *Packt Publishing*

www.PacktPub.com

Support files, eBooks, discount offers, and more

You might want to visit www.PacktPub.com for support files and downloads related to your book.

Did you know that Packt offers eBook versions of every book published, with PDF and ePub files available? You can upgrade to the eBook version at www.PacktPub.com and as a print book customer, you are entitled to a discount on the eBook copy. Get in touch with us at service@packtpub.com for more details.

At www.PacktPub.com, you can also read a collection of free technical articles, sign up for a range of free newsletters, and receive exclusive discounts and offers on Packt books and eBooks.

http://PacktLib.PacktPub.com

Do you need instant solutions to your IT questions? PacktLib is Packt's online digital book library. Here, you can access, read, and search across Packt's entire library of books.

Why subscribe?

- Fully searchable across every book published by Packt
- Copy and paste, print, and bookmark content
- On demand and accessible via web browser

Free access for Packt account holders

If you have an account with Packt at www.PacktPub.com, you can use this to access PacktLib today and view nine entirely free books. Simply use your login credentials for immediate access.

Instant updates on new Packt books

Get notified! Find out when new books are published by following @PacktEnterprise on Twitter, or the *Packt Enterprise* Facebook page.

Table of Contents

Preface

This book covers the use of vSphere Replication and VMware Site Recovery Manager for making your vSphere environment recoverable in the event of a disaster. All the concepts and tasks covered in this book are for vSphere Replication 5.5 and VMware vCenter Site Recovery Manager 5.5.

What this book covers

Chapter 1, Installing and Configuring vCenter Site Recovery Manager (SRM) 5.5, introduces you to the architecture of SRM and also guides you through the process of installing and configuring SRM to leverage array-based replication.

Chapter 2, Creating Protection Groups and Recovery Plans, teaches you how to configure protection for virtual machines by creating Protection Groups and creating an orchestrated runbook with the help of Recovery Plans.

Chapter 3, Testing and Performing a Failover and Failback, teaches you how to test the recovery plans that were created and also perform a Planned Migration, a Failover, and a Failback using them.

Chapter 4, Deploying vSphere Replication 5.5, guides you through the steps required in deploying vSphere Replication Appliances and vSphere Replication Servers.

Chapter 5, Configuring and Using vSphere Replication 5.5, teaches you how to add target sites and enable replication on virtual machines and recover them. It will also teach you to configure vCenter SRM to leverage vSphere Replication engine.

What you need for this book

If you were to follow along with each chapter by practicing the tasks in a lab, then you would need two ESXi hosts, two vCenter Servers, two SRM instances, and two storage array nodes with replication configured between them. This might sound like a lot of hardware, but all you need is VMware Workstation 9.x or 10.x and a Virtual Storage Appliance such as HP Store Virtual 9500 (LeftHand networks). You could get a trial license for HP Store Virtual by registering for one at HP's website. The ESXi hosts, vCenter Servers, vSphere Replication Appliances, SRM Servers, and the storage nodes would be virtual machines that are hosted using VMware Workstation.

Who this book is for

This book is a guide for anyone who is keen on using vSphere Replication or vCenter Site Recovery Manager as a disaster recovery solution. This is an excellent handbook for solution architects, administrators, on-field engineers, and support professionals. Although the book assumes that the reader has some basic knowledge of data center virtualization using VMware vSphere, it can still be a very good reference for anyone who is new to virtualization.

Conventions

In this book, you will find a number of styles of text that distinguish between different kinds of information. Here are some examples of these styles, and an explanation of their meaning.

Code words in text, database table names, folder names, filenames, file extensions, pathnames, dummy URLs, user input, and Twitter handles are shown as follows: "For instance, if you were protecting the SQL Server VMs, then you might name the protection group as `SQL Server Protection Group`."

Any command-line input or output is written as follows:

For instance, to run a batch script in `D:\demoscript.bat`, include the following command:

```
c:\windows\system32\cmd.exe /c d:\demoscript.bat
```

New terms and **important words** are shown in bold. Words that you see on the screen, in menus or dialog boxes for example, appear in the text like this: "Click on **Recovery Plans** on the left pane."

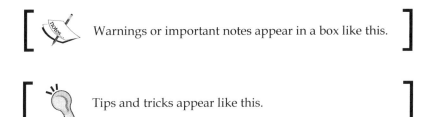

Warnings or important notes appear in a box like this.

Tips and tricks appear like this.

Reader feedback

Feedback from our readers is always welcome. Let us know what you think about this book—what you liked or may have disliked. Reader feedback is important for us to develop titles that you really get the most out of.

To send us general feedback, simply send an e-mail to feedback@packtpub.com, and mention the book title via the subject of your message.

If there is a topic that you have expertise in and you are interested in either writing or contributing to a book, see our author guide on www.packtpub.com/authors.

Customer support

Now that you are the proud owner of a Packt book, we have a number of things to help you to get the most from your purchase.

Errata

Although we have taken every care to ensure the accuracy of our content, mistakes do happen. If you find a mistake in one of our books—maybe a mistake in the text or the code—we would be grateful if you would report this to us. By doing so, you can save other readers from frustration and help us improve subsequent versions of this book. If you find any errata, please report them by visiting http://www.packtpub.com/submit-errata, selecting your book, clicking on the **errata submission form** link, and entering the details of your errata. Once your errata are verified, your submission will be accepted and the errata will be uploaded on our website, or added to any list of existing errata, under the Errata section of that title. Any existing errata can be viewed by selecting your title from http://www.packtpub.com/support.

Piracy

Piracy of copyright material on the Internet is an ongoing problem across all media. At Packt, we take the protection of our copyright and licenses very seriously. If you come across any illegal copies of our works, in any form, on the Internet, please provide us with the location address or website name immediately so that we can pursue a remedy.

Please contact us at `copyright@packtpub.com` with a link to the suspected pirated material.

We appreciate your help in protecting our authors, and our ability to bring you valuable content.

Questions

You can contact us at `questions@packtpub.com` if you are having a problem with any aspect of the book, and we will do our best to address it.

1

Installing and Configuring vCenter Site Recovery Manager (SRM) 5.5

In this chapter, we will cover the following topics:

- What is Site Recovery Manager (SRM)?
- Preparing storage for array-based replication
- Host presentation at protected and recovery sites
- Installing SRM on protected and recovery sites
- Installing SRM plugin for vSphere Client
- Pairing sites
- Installing Storage Replication Adapters (SRA)
- Adding an array manager
- Enabling an array pair
- Configuring placeholder datastores
- Creating resource, folder, and network mappings

Introduction

With today's IT infrastructures, be it virtual or physical, disaster recovery is of prime importance. Any business should be able to continue operating with reduced downtime for its sustainability amongst the competition. It also has a legal obligation towards customers to whom it sold its services. Two of the major factors used to market or sell a service are its High Availability and Recoverability.

Recoverability is the guarantee that the service offered and its data are protected against failures, and High Availability is the guarantee that the service offered would remain operational and the failures are handled in a way that the user of the service would not even know that there was a failure.

There are many ways in which businesses plan and implement disaster recovery. Although important, much of these decisions depend on the budgetary constraints. What turns out to be the most important is the existence of a disaster recovery plan. Gone are those days when you had to wait for a long period of time before all your critical applications were made available at a recovery site. With a lot of automation and scripting, businesses now expect better **Recovery Point Objective (RPO)** and **Recovery Time Objective (RTO)**.

So what exactly are RPO and RTO?

RPO defines the amount of data an organization can afford to lose when measured against time.

RTO defines the amount of downtime the organization can afford for its services before it becomes operational again.

Both RPO and RTO are defined by time. For example, an organization can have an RPO set to 4 hours and RTO set to 1 hour. This means, it can afford to lose up to 4 hours of data, but it can only afford a service downtime up to 1 hour.

RTO only defines the amount of time a service can remain unavailable but doesn't account for the data loss. This is where RPO pitches in. It defines how much data loss can be afforded.

For example, if you were a company hosting an online document format conversion service, then setting a lower RTO value is very important because the customers will prefer access to the service, rather than to the historical data. The RPO value will determine how much historical data you will have to keep.

Both RPO and RTO help an organization to determine the type of backup and DR solution to meet the business requirements.

What is Site Recovery Manager (SRM)?

vCenter **Site Recovery Manager** (**SRM**) is an orchestration software that is used to automate disaster recovery testing and Failover. It can be configured to leverage either vSphere Replication or a supported array-based replication. With SRM, you can create Protection Groups and run Recovery Plans against them. The Recovery Plans can then be used to test the DR setup and perform a planned Failover, or it can be initiated during a disaster recovery. SRM is a not a product that performs an automatic Failover, which means that there is no intelligence built into SRM that would detect a disaster/outage and Failover the VMs. The disaster recovery process should be manually initiated. Hence, it is not a high availability solution; it is purely a tool that orchestrates a Recovery Plan.

Architecture

vCenter Site Recovery Manager is not a tool that works on its own. It needs to talk to other components in the vSphere environment. I will walk you through all the components involved in an environment protected using SRM.

The following are the components that will be involved in an SRM-protected environment:

Protected site	Recovery site
vCenter Server	vCenter Server
SRM instance	SRM instance
Array managers	Array managers
Storage Replication Adapter	Storage Replication Adapter

SRM requires both the protected and recovery sites to be managed by separate instances of the vCenter Server. It also requires an SRM instance at both the sites. SRM's functionalities are currently only available via the vSphere Client and not the vSphere Web Client. Hence, an SRM plugin needs to be installed on the same machine where the vSphere Client is installed. Refer to the following figure:

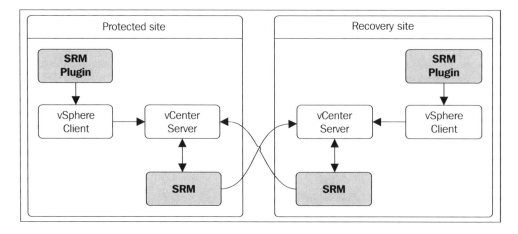

SRM as a solution cannot work on its own. This is because it is only an orchestration tool, and it does not include a replication engine. However, it can leverage either a supported array-based replication or VMware's proprietary replication engine, vSphere Replication. We have separate chapters covering the vSphere Replication.

Array manager

Each SRM instance needs to be configured with an array manager for it to communicate with the storage array. The array manager will detect the storage array using the information you supply to connect to the array. Before you add an array manager, you need to install an array-specific **Storage Replication Adapter (SRA)**. This is because the array manager uses the SRA installed to collect replication information from the array. Refer to the following figure:

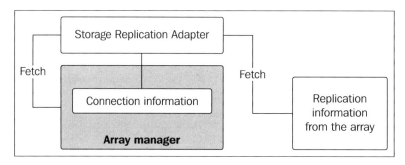

Storage Replication Adapter (SRA)

SRA is a storage vendor component that makes SRM aware of the replication configuration at the array. SRM leverages SRA's ability to gather information regarding the replicated volumes and direction of the replication from the array.

SRM also uses SRA for the following functions:

- Test Failover
- Recovery
- Reprotection

This is illustrated in the following figure:

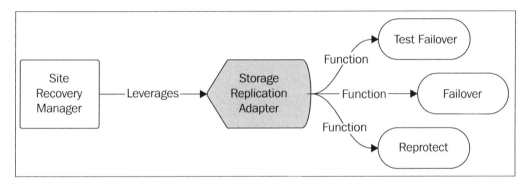

We will learn more about these functions in the next chapter. For now, it is important to understand that SRM requires SRA to be installed for all of its functions leveraging array-based replication.

When all these components are put together, a site protected by SRM will look as is shown in the following figure:

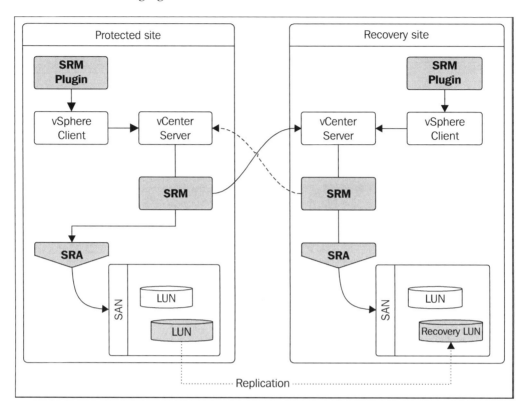

SRM conceptually assumes that both the protected and recovery sites are geographically separated. However, such a separation is not mandatory. You could use SRM to protect a chassis of servers and have another chassis in the same datacenter as the recovery site. Now that we have a brief understanding of the SRM architecture, it is time to learn how to set up these components.

Laying the groundwork for an SRM environment

You will need to perform a set of configuration activities to lay the groundwork for an SRM environment so that it can be used to test or execute the Recovery Plans.

Here is an outline of the tasks that need to be done to form an SRM environment:

- Preparing storage for an array-based replication
- Host presentation (zoning) at the protected and recovery sites
- Installing SRM on both the protected and recovery sites
- Installing the SRM plugin for vSphere Client
- Pairing the SRM instances
- Installing SRA
- Adding array managers
- Enabling array pairs
- Creating resource, folder, and network mappings
- Creating placeholder datastores

Preparing storage for an array-based replication

The first thing that you will need to do is make sure that your array is supported by VMware and licensed for an array-based replication by the array vendor. This is not a VMware license but a licensed feature from the storage vendor.

Now, to enable replication, you have a couple of approaches that you could employ, which are as follows:

Approach-1	Approach-2
• Identify the VMs that you want to protect	• Identify the VMs that you want to protect
• Identify the VMFS datastores the VMs have their files on	• Plan the sizing of a datastore large enough to hold all the identified VMs
• Identify the LUNs corresponding to the already identified datastores	• Create a LUN large enough to host the datastore
• Enable replication on the identified LUNs	• Present the new LUN to the hosts running the identified VM and create a new VMFS volume (datastore) on it
	• Migrate the VMs that you want to protect onto the new datastore
	• Enable replication on the new LUN that corresponds to the new datastore

Approach-1 is used in scenarios where the array does not have the spare capacity to provide a separate LUN to host-protected VMs. This approach adds an administrative overhead if the virtual machines are spread across multiple datastores. It also contributes to wastage of replication bandwidth and storage space since the LUNs that are replicated will contain unprotected virtual machine data.

Approach-2 is used in scenarios where you have ample spare capacity. This approach is the best as it reduces complexity, avoids replication bandwidth wastage, and reduces space wastage, as compared to Approach-1. However, this approach will have an impact on the size of the LUNs required at both the protected and replication sites.

Host presentation (zoning) at the protected and recovery sites

If you are involved in a new implementation, then you will have to plan how the ESXi hosts are zoned to the array at both the protected and recovery sites. This means that LUNs should be correctly zoned at the fabric. The details for protected site and recovery site arrays are as follows:

- At the protected site array, zone the ESXi hosts to communicate with the array and make sure that the LUNs housing the VMs to be protected are assigned to the ESXi hosts

- At the recovery site array, zone the ESXi hosts to the array, but do not map the replica LUNs to the hosts yet

Installing SRM on the protected and recovery sites

VCenter SRM has to be installed at both the protected and recovery sites for the disaster recovery setup to work. The installation process is identical regardless of the site it is being installed on; the only difference is that at each site, you will be registering the SRM installation to the vCenter Server managing that site.

SRM can either be installed on the same machine that has vCenter Server installed or on a different machine. The decision to choose either one of the installation models depends on how you want to size or separate the service-providing machines in your infrastructure. The most common deployment model is to have both vCenter and SRM on the same machine. The rationale behind this is that SRM will not work in a standalone mode; this means that if your vCenter Server goes down, there is no way you could access SRM. Like vCenter Server, SRM can be installed on a physical or virtual machine.

Another factor that you must take into account is the installation of SRA. SRAs have to be installed on the same machine where you already have SRM installed. Some SRAs need a reboot after installation. So, it is important to read through the storage vendor's documentation prior to proceeding to make a deployment choice for SRM. If the vCenter downtime is not feasible, then you will have to consider installing SRM on a separate machine.

Nevertheless, it is important to be aware of the software and hardware requirements of a software installation before it is actually installed. This is to make sure that you don't run into compatibility or supportability issues during the course of using the product. To understand the requirement of SRM, refer to page number 23 in *Chapter 2, Site Recovery Manager System Requirements*, in the *Site Recovery Manager installation and configuration guide for SRM 5.5* document available at `http://pubs.vmware.com/ srm-55/topic/com.vmware.ICbase/PDF/srm-install-config-5-5.pdf`.

The following flowchart depicts the processes involved in installing vCenter SRM:

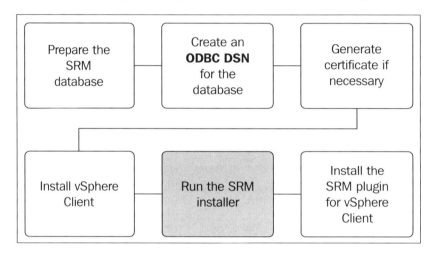

Performing the SRM installation

Let's assume that the SRM database and the 64-bit DSN have already been created. We will delve directly into the installation procedure using the SRM installer.

Before you begin, you will need to download the SRM installation bundle from the VMware website. It can be downloaded by navigating to `www.vmware.com` and then to the **vCenter Site Recovery Manager** option in the **Downloads** menu. You need to log in to your `my.vmware.com` account before you download the executable.

The following procedure will guide you through the SRM installation wizard:

1. Double-click on the downloaded executable to load the installer.

2. On the welcome screen of the installation wizard, click on **Next** to continue.

3. Choose a destination folder for the installer to place the files. The default location is `C:\Program Files\VMware\VMware vCenter Site Recovery Manager\`. You can change this by clicking on the **Change** button. For now, I have chosen to leave the default in place. Click on **Next** to continue.

4. On the next screen, you will be prompted to install the vSphere Replication UI plugin for SRM. You can choose to install or not install the plugin at this stage. Since we are not discussing vSphere Replication in this chapter, I have selected **Do not install vSphere Replication** as the option. Click on **Next** to continue.

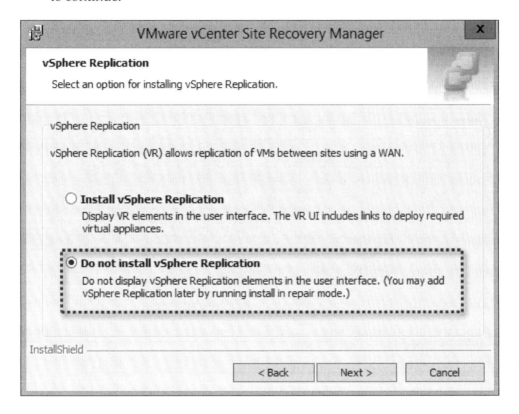

5. On the next screen, provide the FQDN/IP and the credentials of the vCenter Server; the SRM instance should also be registered. Use of a separate service account, instead of the built-in administrator account, is recommended. In most cases where SRM is currently being installed, it is the local vCenter Server managing the site. Click on **Next** to continue.

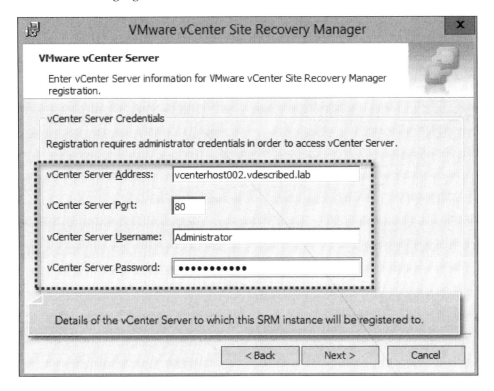

6. You will then be prompted to a certificate source. Here, you can either let the installer generate a certificate, or you can supply a certificate file generated by a certificate authority.

7. The options available are as follows:

   ○ **Automatically generate a certificate**
   ○ **Use a PKCS#12 certificate file**

8. Make a selection of your choice and click on **Next** to continue.

   Here, we have chosen to let the installer generate a new certificate. Use the second option if you already have a certificate file from your certificate authority. VMware recommends using CA-signed certificates for all its products.

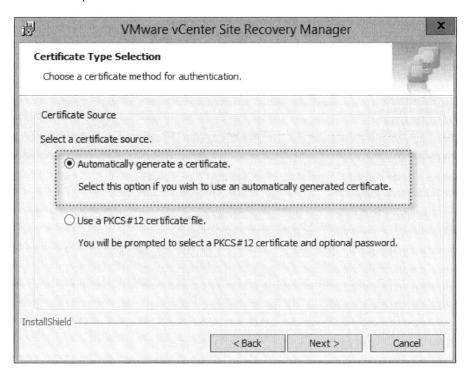

9. On the next screen, supply the details (organization and organization unit) for the certificate generation, and then click on **Next** to continue. You will be prompted for this information only if you have chosen to automatically generate a certificate.

10. Supply a local site name, two e-mail addresses of the administrators who need to be notified of any event, and the IP address of the machine where we will install SRM. The local site name can be any name that you supply. In this case, I have used the name of the vCenter Server that is managing the site. The site name can be changed by going to the **Advanced Settings** tab of the site post installation. Click on **Next** to continue.

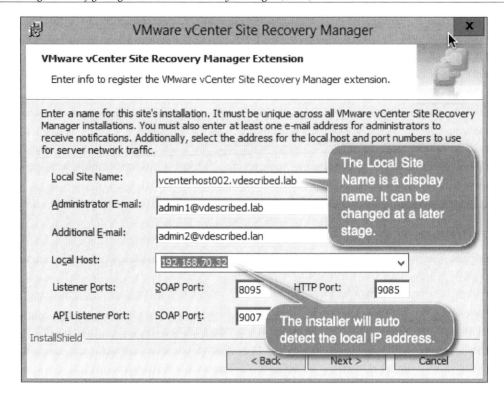

11. Now, you will be prompted to supply the details of the database that you previously created for SRM.

12. The following details are needed to proceed further:

    ° The name of the 64-bit DSN that is configured to connect to the SRM database.

    ° The database user credentials, which could be a user that you created manually at the database server for the SRM database. Although, in this example, I have used the sa credentials, it is not a recommended practice to expose the sa credentials. In most environments, the sa account is used by the database administrator. Consider using a separate service account.

13. Supply the details and click on **Next** to continue.

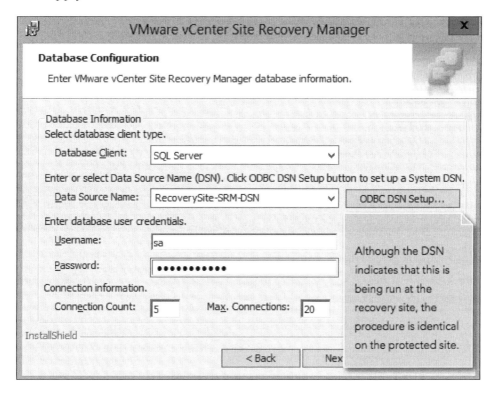

14. On the **Ready to install the Program** screen, click on **Install** to begin the installation.

15. Once the installation is complete, click on **Finish** to exit the installer.

Installing the SRM plugin for vSphere Client

The SRM functions are exposed in the vSphere Client UI with the help of the SRM plugin. The SRM installer does not install this plugin. This is because it is a plugin for the vSphere Client and not the vCenter Server. The plugin needs to be installed separately on the machine where you have vSphere Client installed.

This is how you do it:

1. Connect to vCenter Server using vSphere Client.

2. Navigate to the **Manage Plug-ins** option in the **Plug-ins** tab, as shown in the following screenshot:

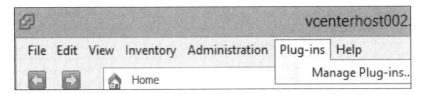

3. In the **Plug-in Manager** window, the SRM plugin should be listed under the **Available Plug-ins** category.

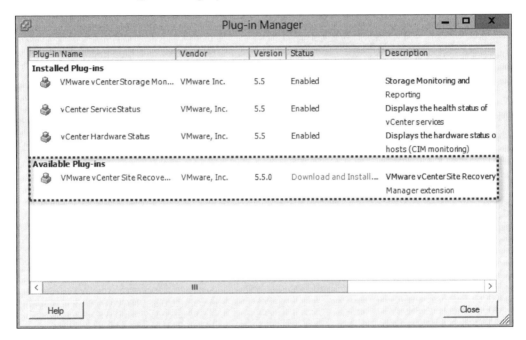

4. Click on the **Download and Install** link to fetch and install the SRM Plugin. The plugin installation is pretty straightforward.

5. Once the installation is complete, the vCenter inventory home page should list **Site Recovery** under **Solutions and Applications**.

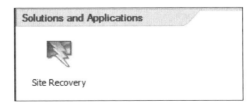

Pairing sites

Once SRM is installed on both the sites, the next step is to pair the sites together. The pairing process establishes a connection between the vCenter Servers at the protected and recovery sites, which in turn makes the SRM instances at both the sites aware of its counterpart at the other site (protected/recovery). Without the sites being paired, we can't proceed further with the configuration of the DR setup.

This is how the sites are paired:

1. Connect to the protected/recovery site vCenter Server using vSphere Client.
2. Navigate to the inventory home page and click on **Site Recovery**.
3. Click on **Sites** in the left pane.
4. Right-click on the local site listed, and click on **Configure Connection** to bring up the configure connection wizard. Refer to the following screenshot:

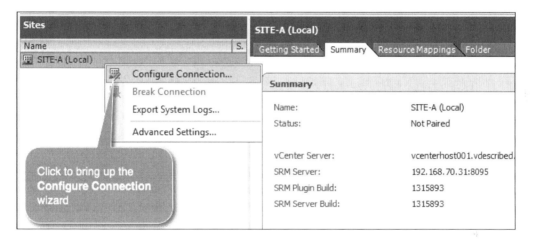

5. In the **Configure Connection** wizard, supply the FQDN of the remote vCenter Server and click on **Next** to continue. Accept any subsequent certificate warnings.

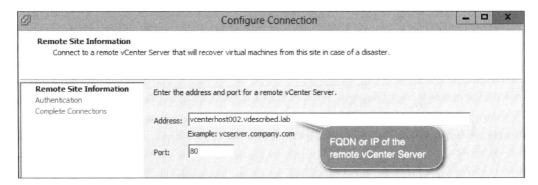

6. Furnish the administrator credentials, and click on **Next**. Accept any subsequent certificate warnings.

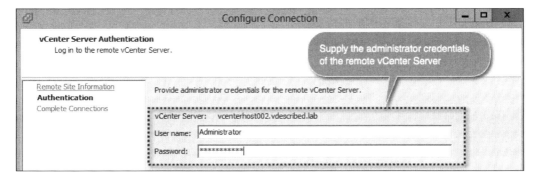

7. This will begin the pairing process, which will establish a connection with the remote vCenter Server and SRM, and also establish reciprocity. Click on **Finish** to exit the wizard.

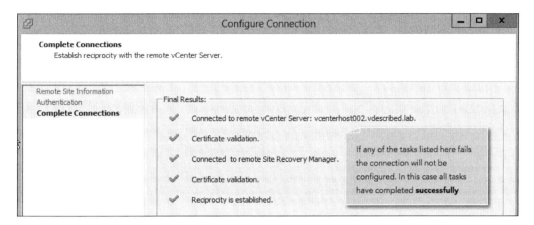

8. Once you exit the wizard, you will be prompted again for the administrator credentials of the remote vCenter Server. Enter the credentials and click on **OK**. Ignore any subsequent certificate warnings. Refer to the following screenshot:

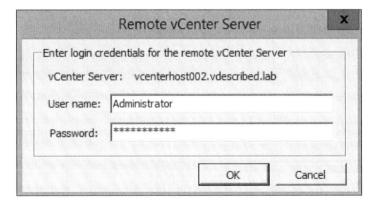

9. You should see both the sites listed under the **Sites** pane now:

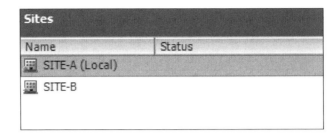

Keep in mind that the pairing is done only from one of the sites. This is because the pairing process establishes reciprocity by configuring the connection in the reverse direction as well. However, when you open the site recovery solution at the remote vCenter Server, you will be prompted to enter the administrator credentials of the other site.

Installing Storage Replication Adapters

Once you have the SRM instances installed and paired, the next step is to install the Storage Replication Adapters. SRAs are coded and provided by the storage vendors. VMware certifies the SRAs and posts them as compatible with the SRM.

Downloading SRA

The certified versions of SRA can be downloaded directly from VMware's website. Keep in mind that most vendors publish the updated versions of SRA at their website before it is certified by VMware. Since SRA is a vendor-supported component, you can choose to install the latest version available from the vendor, if that is known to fix a problem you are dealing with.

This is how you can download an SRA:

1. Go to VMware's website at www.vmware.com.

2. Navigate to the **vCenter Site Recovery Manager** option in **Downloads** under the **Product Downloads** category.

3. Once you are at the download page for vCenter SRM, click on the **Go to Downloads** hyperlink listed against SRA.

4. At the **Download Storage Replication Adapters for VMware vCenter Site Recovery Manager** page, you will see a list of all the certified SRAs. Click on the **Download Now** button corresponding to the needed SRA.

Installing SRA

Once downloaded, the SRA component has to be installed on both the sites. In most cases, the SRA installation is pretty simple and straightforward, but this can be different from vendor to vendor. You need to refer to the vendor documentation for the installation procedure.

Once the installation is complete, follow this procedure to discover the installed SRA component:

1. Connect to the protected/recovery site of vCenter Server using vSphere Client.
2. Navigate to the inventory home page and click on **Site Recovery**.
3. Click on **Array Managers** in the left pane and navigate to the **SRAs** tab.
4. In the **SRAs** tab, click on **Rescan SRAs** to discover the installed SRA.
5. Repeat the procedure at the recovery site as well.

Adding an array manager

Once you have the SRA installed and discovered at both the sites, you will need to add an array manager at both the sites. An array manager is required to discover the replicated LUNs and perform other storage operations initiated by SRM.

This is how you add an array manager:

1. Connect to the protected/recovery site of vCenter Server using vSphere Client.
2. Navigate to the vCenter Server's inventory home page and click on **Site Recovery**.

3. Click on **Array Managers** in the left pane, select the site, and click on
Add Array Manager to bring up the **Add Array Manager** wizard,
as shown in the following screenshot:

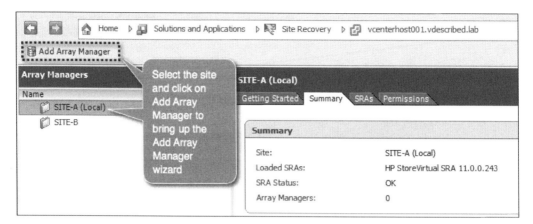

4. In the wizard, supply a **Display Name** for the array manager and an **SRA
Type**. The SRA type value field will be prepopulated with the SRA that is
already installed. Click on **Next** to continue.

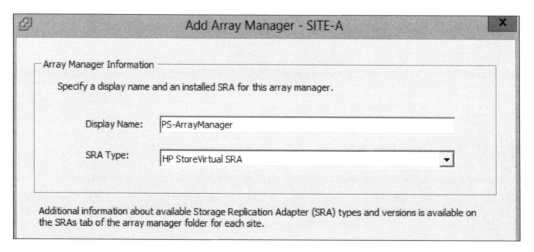

5. On the next screen, you will be prompted to enter the IP address of the storage node or a management server, which does the array management. Keep in mind that the information this screen prompts for differs from array to array and from vendor to vendor. It is purely dependent on what SRA is being used. Here in this example, I use the HP StoreVirtual (LeftHand) SRA and what I have entered as the Virtual IP (VIP) of the cluster the **Node Storage Module** (**NSM**) is part of. If I don't use this, all the NSMs in the cluster are involved in the replication of SRM, and then I can supply the IP addresses of the involved NSMs separated by a comma.

6. Supply the details and click on **Next** to continue. Refer to the following screenshot:

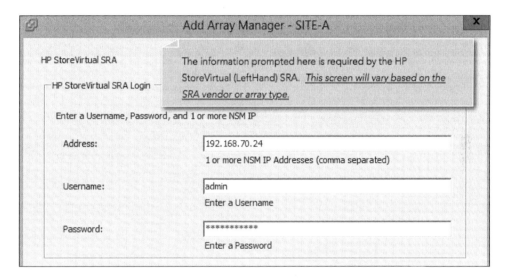

7. The next screen will read **Success** if the array managers are added successfully. Click on **Finish** to exit the wizard.

8. Repeat the same procedure on the recovery site as well.

9. Once done, the **Array Managers** for both the sites should be listed, as shown in the following screenshot:

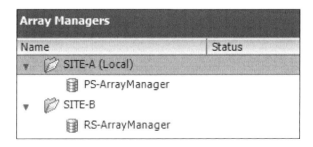

Enabling an array pair

An array pair shows the replication relationship between two arrays. Before you enable an array pair, you need SRA installed and the array manager added at both the sites. For the array manager to detect an array pair, there should be a replication schedule already created between the arrays. Refer to the vendor documentation to understand what a replication schedule means for the vendor's array and the procedure to create it.

This is how you enable an array pair:

1. Make sure that there is a replication schedule enabled between the two arrays.

2. Navigate to the vCenter Server's inventory home page and click on **Site Recovery**.

3. Click on **Array Managers** in the left pane.

4. Select an added **Array Manager** (local or remote), and click on **Refresh** to discover an array pair, as shown in the following screenshot:

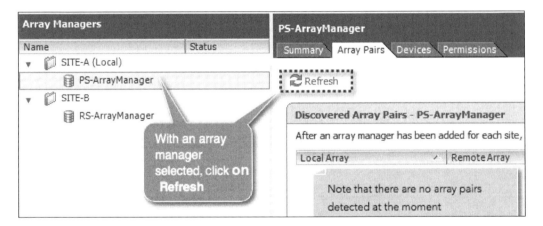

5. If the **Refresh** action discovers an array pair, the array pair will be listed. The **Refresh** action has to be done at both of the sites.

6. Array pairs discovered are not enabled by default. To enable an array pair, select an array pair and click on **Enable**. This operation has to done at only one of the sites.

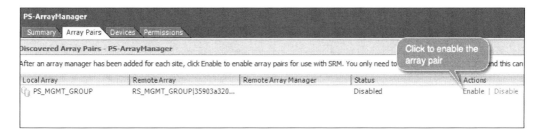

7. When an array pair is enabled, it tries to discover the devices (LUNs) for which a replication schedule is enabled at the array. Keep in mind that not all devices with a replication schedule are displayed as a device for the array pair; only the ones that are presented to a host at the protected site are displayed. To view the detected and filtered replication-enabled devices with the array manager selected, navigate to the **Devices** tab and click on **Refresh**, as shown in the following screenshot:

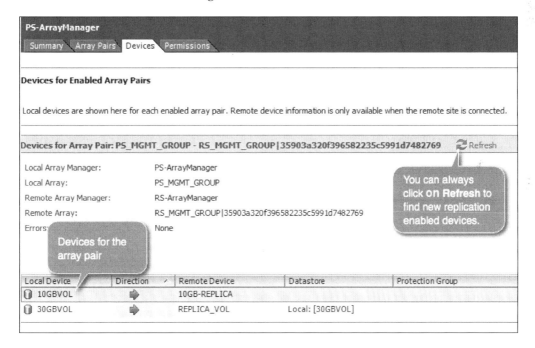

Configuring placeholder datastores

In the next chapter, you will learn how to create Protection Groups. For every virtual machine that becomes part of a Protection Group, SRM creates a shadow virtual machine. A placeholder datastore is used to store the files for the shadow virtual machines. The datastore used for this purpose should be accessible to all the hosts in the datacenter/cluster serving the role of a recovery-host. We will learn more about Protection Groups and shadow virtual machines in the next chapter. For now, understand that configuring placeholder datastores is an essential step in forming an SRM environment.

Assuming that each of these paired sites is geographically separated, each site will have its own placeholder datastore. The following figure shows the site and placeholder datastore relationship:

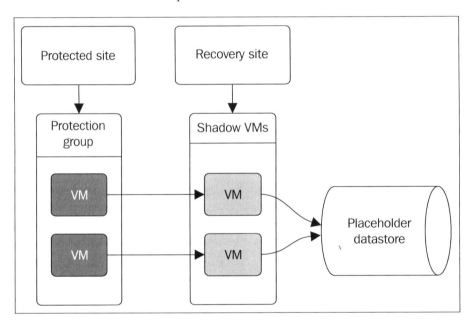

This is how you configure placeholder datastores:

1. Navigate to vCenter Server's inventory home page and click on **Site Recovery**.

2. Click on **Sites** in the left pane and select a site. Navigate to the **Placeholder Datastores** tab and click on **Configure Placeholder Datastore**, as shown in the following screenshot:

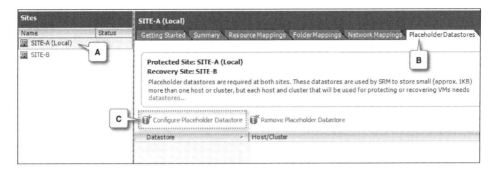

3. In the **Configure Placeholder Datastore** window, select an appropriate datastore and click on **OK**. To confirm the selection, exit the window.

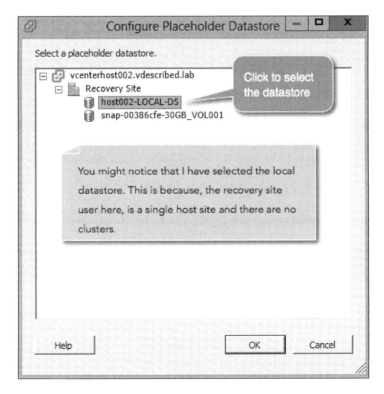

4. Now, the **Placeholder Datastores** tab should show the configured placeholder. Refer to the following screenshot:

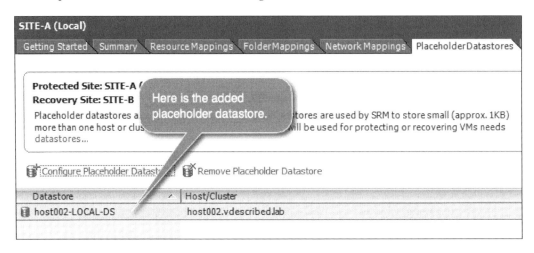

5. If you plan to configure a Failback, repeat the procedure in the recovery site.

Creating resource, folder, and network mappings

Creating resource, folder, and network mappings facilitates further orchestration of the Recovery Plan that will be executed for either a Planned Migration or a Failover. Without these mappings, you won't be able to configure protection on the virtual machines, and the protection status will indicate that these mapping are missing. We will learn more about Protection Groups in the next chapter.

Apart from being a requirement for creating Protection Groups, there are other use cases as well. The following table shows a few common ones:

Use cases	Mapping to use
If the designated recovery site runs other workload, then you may want to create a separate folder for the VMs from the protected site.	Folder mappings
If there is a separate cluster/resource pool at the recovery site to host, the VMs are recovered from the protected site.	Resource mappings
If there are vSwitch/DSwitch port groups at the recovery site for the recovered VMs, we use the network mapping.	Network mappings

Resource mappings

We need to provide a correlation between the compute resource containers on both the sites. The compute resource containers are cluster, resource pool, and ESXi host. This is achieved with the help of resource mappings.

Resource mappings respect the presence of these containers, which means that if there is a cluster or resource pool at the site, the ESXi hosts are not made available as a selectable compute container.

This is how you configure resource mappings:

1. Navigate to vCenter Server's inventory home page and click on **Site Recovery**.

2. Click on **Sites** in the left pane, select a site, and navigate to the **Resource Mappings** tab. Select the resource container (a cluster, resource pool, or host) you want to map, and click on **Configure Mapping** to bring up the **Mapping** window. Refer to the following screenshot:

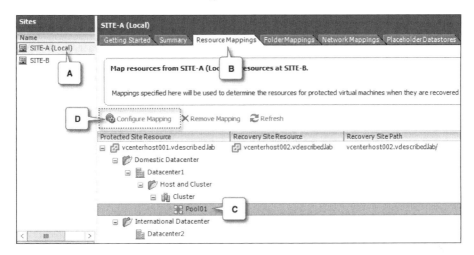

3. In the **Mapping** window, browse the resource inventory of the recovery site, select the destination resource container (a cluster, resource pool, or host), and click on **OK** to confirm.

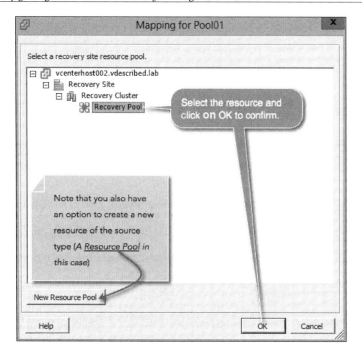

4. The **Resource Mapping** tab should now show the mapped **Recovery Site Resource**.

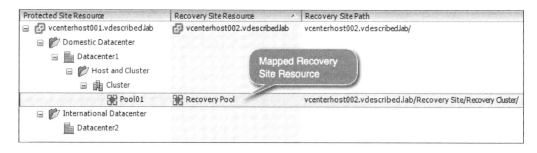

Folder mappings

Folders are inventory containers that can only be created using vCenter Server. They are used to group inventory objects of the same type for easier management.

There are different types of folders. The folder type is determined by the inventory-hierarchy level they are created at. The folder names are as follows:

- Datacenter folder
- Hosts and clusters folder
- Virtual machine and template folder
- Network folder
- Storage folder

The vSphere Web Client provides UI menu options to create a folder of the following types, without needing to navigate to an appropriate inventory-hierarchy level to create them:

- Hosts and clusters folder
- Network folders
- Storage folder
- Virtual machine and template folder

In the case of SRM folder mappings, we will deal with only virtual machine folders and its parent datacenter. You will not be able to configure mapping for any of the other folder types.

This is how you configure folder mapping:

1. Navigate to vCenter Server's inventory home page and click on **Site Recovery**.
2. Click on **Sites** in the left pane, select a site, and navigate to the **Folder Mappings** tab. Select the virtual machine folder that you want to map, and click on **Configure Mapping** to bring up the **Mapping** window, as shown in the following screenshot:

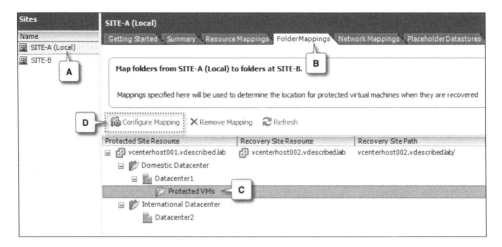

3. In the **Mapping for Protected VMs** window, browse the virtual machine folder inventory of the recovery site, select the destination folder, and click on **OK** to confirm.

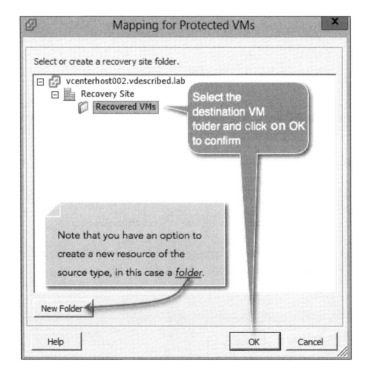

It is important to make sure that the parent datacenter of which the virtual machine folder is part of is mapped as well. The procedure to configure mapping is the same.

4. The **Folder Mapping** tab should now show the mapped recovery site folder. Refer to the following screenshot:

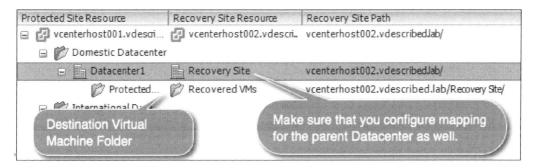

Network mappings

Network configuration at the protected and recovery sites need not be identical. Network mappings provide a method to form a correlation between the port groups (standard or distributed) of the protected and recovery steps.

Let's say we have a port group with the name VM Network at the protected site, and it is mapped to a port group with the name Recovery Network at the recovery site. In this case, a virtual machine that is connected to VM Network will be reconfigured to use the Recovery Network when failed over.

This is how you configure network mappings:

1. Navigate to vCenter Server's inventory home page and click on **Site Recovery**.
2. Click on **Sites** in the left pane, select a site, and navigate to the **Network Mappings** tab. Select the port group (standard/distributed) that you want to map, and click on **Configure Mapping** to bring up the **Mapping** window, as shown in the following screenshot:

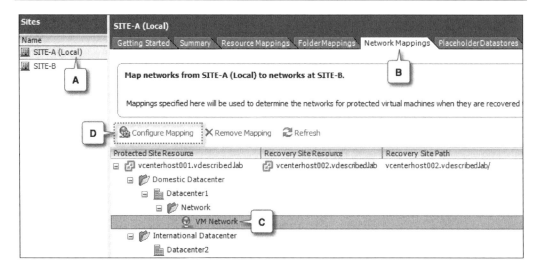

3. In the **Mapping for VM Network** window, browse the network inventory of the recovery site, select the destination port group, and click on **OK** to confirm.

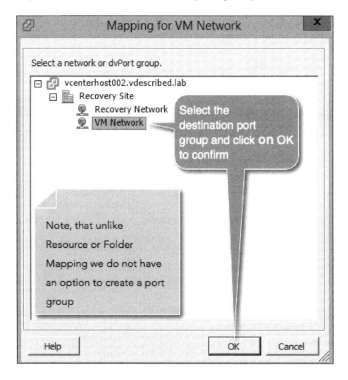

4. The **Network Mappings** tab should now show the mapped recovery site port group, as shown in the following screenshot:

Virtual machine swap file location

With SRM implementations, there is a common argument about the placement of the virtual machine swap files. Some would suggest maintaining a separate datastore for the virtual machine swap files, while some are against it. Before we try to understand the rationale behind either of the design choices, it is important to know what a virtual machine swap file is.

Every virtual machine will have a swap file (.vswp). This swap file is created every time a virtual machine is powered on. The size of the swap file is equal to the size of the memory assigned to the virtual machine, unless there is a reservation. If there is a memory reservation, then the size of the swap file will be equal to the size of the unreserved memory. Although rare, some environments use limits on memory as well.

So, the ideal formula to calculate the size of the swap file is as follows:

Swap file size = memory limit – memory reservation

The default memory reservation is 0 MB, and the default limit is equal to the configured size of the memory. By default, the swap file is stored along with the virtual machine in its working directory.

Design choice 1 – separate datastore for the swap files

The rationale is that the swap file is created every time a virtual machine is powered on. Since the VM will be powered on at the recovery site, the swap file will be created at that time. Hence, there is no need to replicate the swap files. The following table illustrates the pros and cons of this:

Pros	Cons
Swap file replication, if avoided, can reduce the bandwidth utilization for storage replication.	Single point of failure.
Reduces the need for the storage space at the recovery site, which otherwise would be needed for the swap files.	The swap location should be chosen at a per-host level; this would mean a lot of manual work in a large environment.
	Need to accommodate a separate large LUN; this could affect the available spare capacity of the array.

Design choice 2 – store the swap files in the virtual machines' working directory

The rationale is that apart from reduced replication bandwidth usage, there is no real advantage of maintaining a separate datastore for the swap files. Most SRM implementations will already have made sure that there will be more than enough bandwidth to make storage replication feasible. Also, not all virtual machines frequently use the swap files, unless the vSphere environment is oversubscribed and the virtual machines are frequently contending for memory resources. In most cases, the swap files will be replicated during the initial sync. Subsequent synchronizations will include swap files created consequent to power off and power on operations. Keep in mind that a guest OS reboot will not trigger the recreation of the swap files. The following table illustrates the pros and cons of this:

Pros	Cons
No administrative overhead, which would otherwise be needed to configuring a swap datastore per host.	Bandwidth wastage, due to the replication of the swap files.
No single point of failure.	Space wastage at the recovery site, which can otherwise be avoided if the swap files are not duplicated onto the replica LUNs.

 The design choices and the rationale behind them can vary depending on the environment you are dealing with. The rationales are only guidelines.

Summary

In this chapter, we learned what VMware vCenter SRM is and how it can be installed and configured to lay the groundwork for any SRM environment. In the next chapter, we will learn how to enable protection of the virtual machine workload by creating Protection Groups and Recovery Plans.

2

Creating Protection Groups and Recovery Plans

In the previous chapter, we learned how to install SRM and configure it and also how to lay the groundwork for an SRM-protected environment. We learned how to create resources, folder, and network mappings and configure placeholder datastores and array managers.

In this chapter, we will cover the following topics:

- Creating Protection Groups
- Creating Recovery Plans

Once you have done the groundwork required to form an SRM-protected environment, the next step is to grant protection to the virtual machines. Before we delve into the procedural steps involved in protecting virtual machines, it is very important to understand a couple of basic concepts such as datastore and Protection Groups.

Datastore groups

A datastore group is a container that aggregates one or more replication-enabled datastores. The datastore groups are created by SRM and cannot be manually altered. A replication-enabled datastore is a datastore who's LUN has a replication schedule enabled at the array.

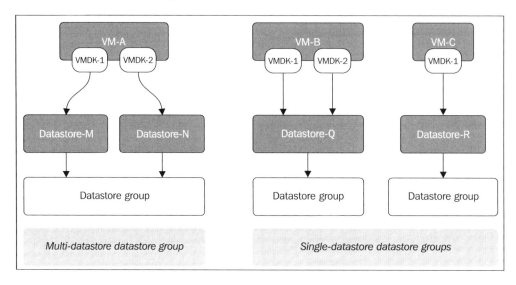

A datastore group will contain only a single datastore if the datastore doesn't store files of virtual machines from other datastores. See the preceding single-datastore datastore group conceptual diagram.

A datastore group can also contain more than one datastore. SRM aggregates multiple datastores into a single group if they have virtual machines whose files are distributed onto these datastores. For example, if VM-A has two VMDKs placed on datastores Datastore-M and Datastore-N each, and then both these datastores become part of the same datastore group. These datastore groups further aid in the creation of Protection Groups.

Protection Groups

Unlike **vSphere Replication**, SRM cannot enable protection on individual virtual machines. All the virtual machines that are hosted on the datastores in a datastore group are protected. Meaning, with SRM, protection is enabled at the datastore group level. This is because, with an array-based replication, the LUNs backing the datastores are replicated. The array doesn't know which VMs are hosted on the datastore. It just replicates the LUN, block by block. So, at the SRM layer, the protection is enabled at the datastore level. In a way, a Protection Group is nothing but a software construct to which datastore groups are added, which in turn includes all the VMs stored on them in the Protection Group.

When creating a Protection Group, you will have to choose the datastore groups that will be included. Keep in mind that you cannot individually select the datastores in a datastore group. If it were ever allowed to do so, then you will have virtual machines with not all of its files protected. Let's assume that you have a virtual machine, VM-A, with two disks (VMDK-1 and VMDK-2) placed on two different datastores. Let's also say VMDK-1 is on Datastore-X and VMDK-2 is on Datastore-Y. When creating a Protection Group, if you were allowed to select the individual datastores and if you choose only one of them, then you will leave the remaining disks of the VM unprotected. Hence, SRM doesn't allow selecting individual datastores from a datastore group as a measure to prevent such a scenario. The following diagram shows the modified conceptual structure of the datastore group:

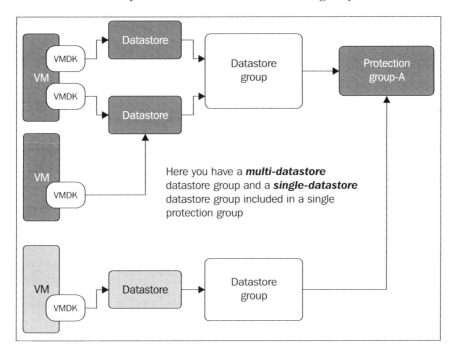

Here you have a **multi-datastore** datastore group and a **single-datastore** datastore group included in a single protection group

Here, even though we have both the datastore groups included in the same Protection Group, **Protection Group-A**, it is possible to form separate Protection Groups for each of the datastore groups.

 Note that a datastore group cannot be a part of two Protection Groups at the same time.

Creating a Protection Group

A Protection Group is created in the SRM UI at the protected site. The following procedure will guide you through the steps required to create a Protection Group:

1. Navigate to the vCenter Server's inventory home and click on **Site Recovery**.

2. Click on **Protection Groups** in the left pane of the window.

3. Click on **Create Protection Group** to bring up the **Create Protection Group** wizard as shown in the following screenshot:

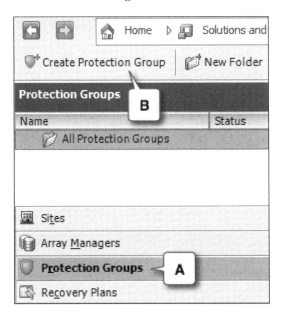

4. In the wizard, make sure the site that you want to protect is selected.

    Keep in mind that the local site (the one that you're locked into) is always selected as the **Protected Site**, as shown in the following screenshot. In case you are using the SRM UI from the **Recovery Site**, you have to manually select the protected site. If the wizard shows more than one array pair, make sure you select the correct one to proceed.

    Click on **Next** to continue.

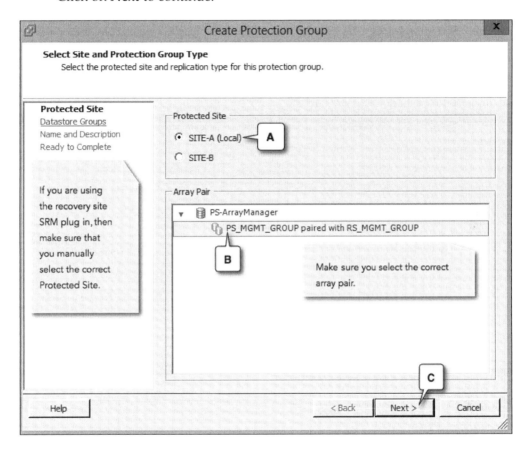

5. On the next screen, choose a datastore group that you would like to protect. When you select a datastore group, the bottom pane will list all the VMs hosted on the datastores in the group. You cannot individually select the VMs though. Although I have selected only a single datastore group, we can select multiple datastore groups to become part of the Protection Group.

   Click on **Next** to continue as shown in the following screenshot:

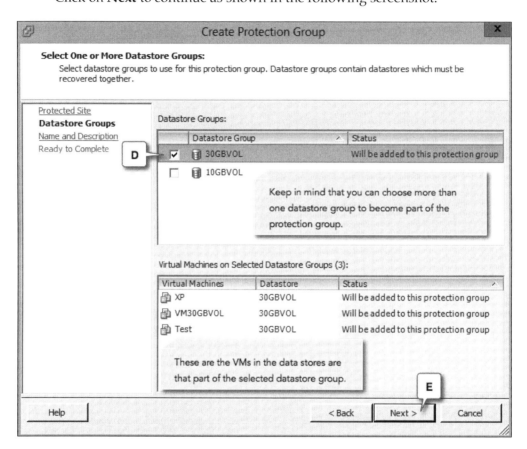

6. In the next screen, provide the **Protection Group Name** and an optional description, and click on **Next** to continue.

   The **Protection Group Name** can be any name that you would prefer to identify the Protection Group with. The common naming convention is to indicate the type or purpose of the VMs. This is because, in most cases, the VMs serving a common purpose or VMs of the same type/priority in an SRM-protected environment are segregated onto separate datastores to aid easier management of the Protection Groups.

7. For instance, if you were protecting the SQL Server VMs, then you might name the Protection Group as `SQL Server Protection Group`; or, if it were to be a set of hyphenate VMs, you may name it as `High Priority VMs Protection Group`.

8. On the **Ready to Complete** screen, as shown in the following screenshot, review the wizard options selected and click on **Finish** to create a Protection Group:

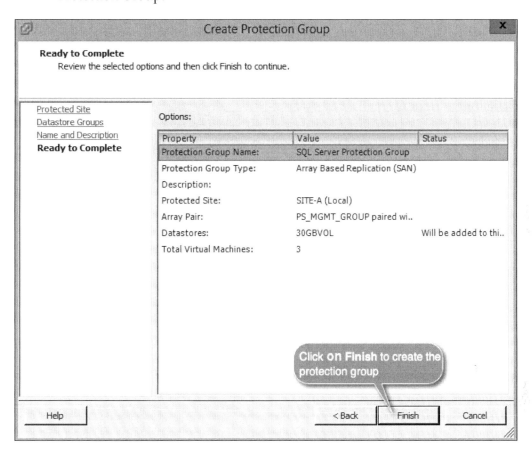

So, what exactly happens when you create a Protection Group?

When you create a Protection Group, it enables protection on all the VMs in the chosen datastore group and creates shadow VMs at the recovery site. In detail, this means that at the protected site vCenter Server, you should see a **Create Protection Group** task complete; subsequently a **Protect VM** task completes successfully for each of the VMs in the Protection Group. See the following screenshot for reference:

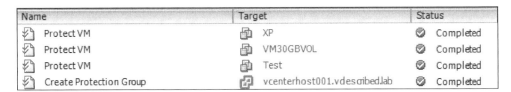

At the recovery site of the vCenter Server, you should see the **Create Protection Group**, **Protect VM** (one for each VM), **Create virtual machine** (one for each VM), and **Recompute Datastore Groups** tasks completed successfully.

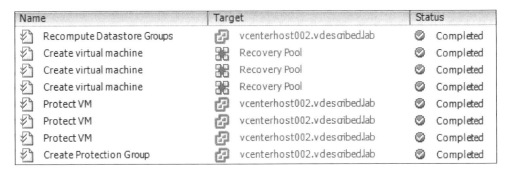

As shown in the following screenshot, the shadow VMs appear in the vCenter Server's inventory at the recovery site:

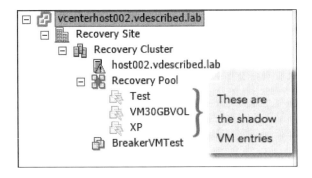

As they are solely placeholders, you cannot perform any power operations on it. There are other operations that are possible but are not recommended. Hence, a warning will be displayed, requesting a confirmation, as shown in the following screenshot:

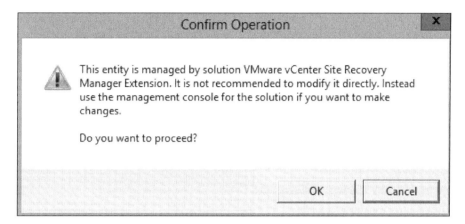

The placeholder datastores will only have the configuration file (.vmx), teaming configuration file (.vmxf), and a snapshot metadata file (.vmsd) for each VM.

These files will be automatically deleted when you delete the Protection Group.

Recovery Plans

Recovery Plans are created at the recovery site so that they are accessible and can be run from the recovery site when there is a disaster at the protected site. A Recovery Plan is executed to Failover the virtual machine workload that was running at the protected site to the recovery site. It can also be used to perform Planned Migrations. A Recovery Plan is a series of configuration steps that has to be performed to Failover the protected virtual machines to the recovery site.

A Recovery Plan should be associated with at least one Protection Group.

Creating a Recovery Plan

Once you have Protection Groups created, the next step would be to create a Recovery Plan for these Protection Groups. The Recovery Plan should be created at the recovery site SRM. This is because, in the event of a disaster, the protected site may become inaccessible. Hence, for very obvious reasons, a Recovery Plan is always created at the recovery site. The following steps show you how to create a Recovery Plan:

1. Navigate to the vCenter Server's inventory home and click on **Site Recovery**.

2. Click on **Recovery Plans [A]** on the left pane.

3. Click on **Create Recovery Plan [B]** to bring up the **Create Recovery Plan** wizard as shown in the following screenshot:

4. In the **Create Recovery Plan** wizard, select the **Recovery Site** and click on **Next** to continue. If the Recovery Plan wizard is initiated at a site, then the wizard will select the other site in the site pair as the recovery site. For example, if you were to initiate the Recovery Plan wizard at SITE-A, then the wizard will autoselect SITE-B as the recovery site and vice versa. Refer to the following screenshot:

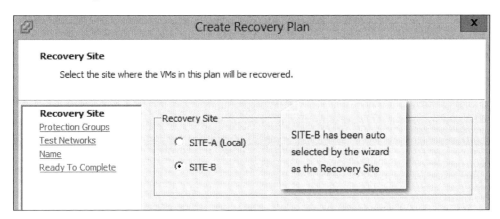

5. As shown in the following screenshot, select the Protection Group that you would like to use and click on **Next** to continue:

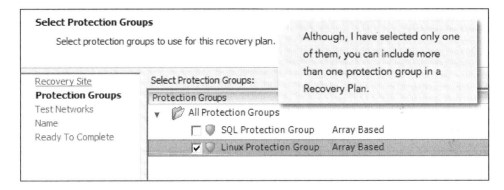

6. In the next wizard screen, click on **Test Networks**. The test networks are set to **Auto** by default. The Auto networks are isolated bubble networks and don't connect to any physical network. They are used when testing a Recovery Plan. We will discuss more about how to test a Recovery Plan and the use of bubble networks in *Chapter 3, Testing and Performing a Failover and Failback*. So unless you have manually created an isolated test network port group at the recovery site, you can leave it at the **Auto** setting. Click on **Next** to continue:

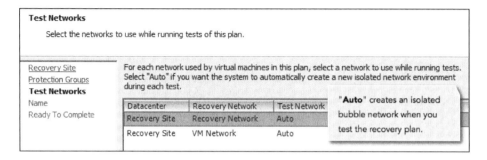

7. In the next screen, enter a **Recovery Plan Name** and an optional **Description** and click on **Next** to continue. The Recovery Plan name can be any name of your choice.

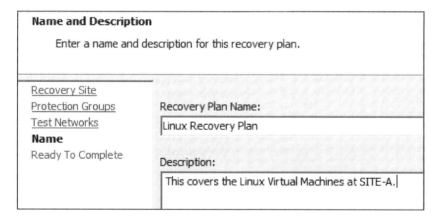

8. In the **Ready to Complete** window, click on **Finish** to create the Recovery Plan.

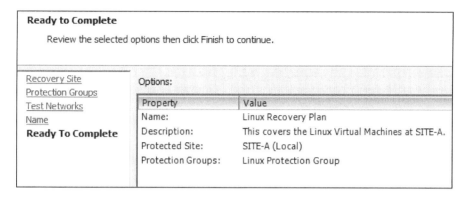

9. You should see the **Create Recovery Plan** task completed successfully in the **Recent Tasks** pane.

Summary

In this chapter, we learned how to create Protection Groups and create Recovery Plans for them. In the next chapter, we learn how to test the Recovery Plans, execute a Failover, reprotect, and a Failback.

3

Testing and Performing a Failover and Failback

In the previous chapter, we learned how to create Protection Groups and Recovery Plans. As discussed, Recovery Plans are nothing but a previously created workflow for the recovery of a failed site. In this chapter, we will learn how to test Recovery Plans that are already created, how to use them to perform a Failover, panned migration, reprotect, and Failback.

The following is a list of topics that will be covered in this chapter:

- Testing a Recovery Plan
- Performing a Planned Migration
- Performing a disaster recovery (Failover)
- Reprotecting a site
- Failback to the protected site
- Configuring VM recovery properties

Testing a Recovery Plan

A Recovery Plan should be tested for its readiness to make sure that it would work as expected in the event of a real disaster. Most organizations periodically review and update their recovery runbook to make sure that they have an optimized, working plan for a recovery.

With SRM, the testing of a Recovery Plan can now be automated. It is important to understand the workflow involved in testing a Recovery Plan before we delve into details of what really happens in the background.

The following steps will guide you through the procedure for testing an already-existing Recovery Plan:

1. Navigate to the vCenter Server's inventory home page and click on **Site Recovery**.

2. Click on **Recovery Plans** on the left pane.

3. Click on the Recovery Plan that you want to test and click on the **Test** toolbar item to bring up the **Test** wizard, as shown in the following screenshot:

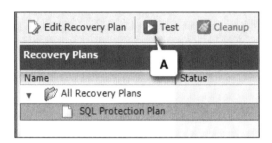

4. As shown in the following screenshot, the first screen of the wizard will indicate which of the sites have been designated as the protected and recovery sites, the site connection status, and the number of VMs protected:

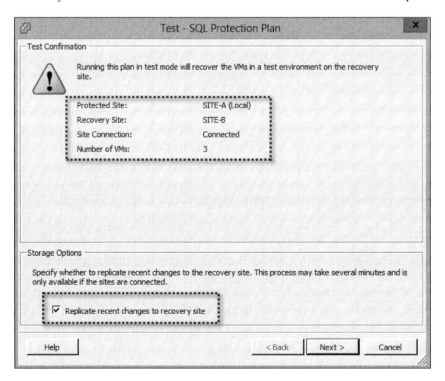

By default, the storage option **Replicate the recent changes to the recovery site** is selected. I would recommend not deselecting this option because we replicate the recent changes during a Planned Migration. So, it is important that the ability of the array to respond to a nonscheduled replication request is tested. However, we might not need to do this if the replication is synchronous. Click on **Next** to continue.

5. The next screen will summarize the selected options as shown in the following screenshot. Review them and click on **Start** to initiate the test:

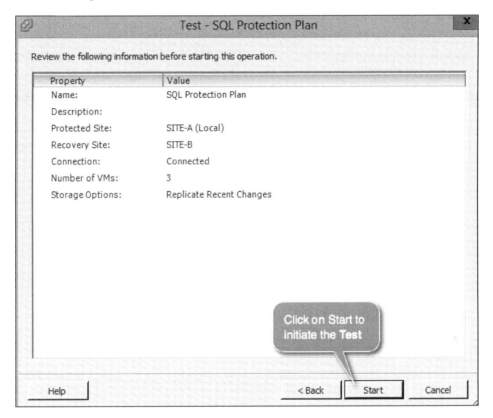

6. You should now see a **Test Recovery Plan** task in the **Recent Tasks** pane. Navigate to the **Recovery Steps** tab to watch the progress of the test as shown in the following screenshot:

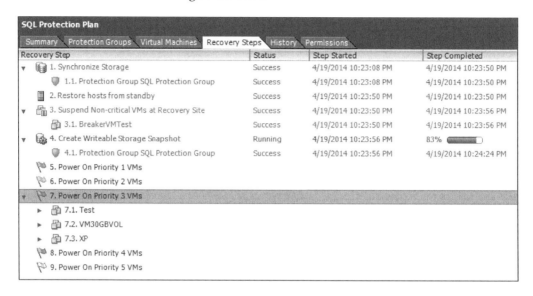

7. Once the test completes successfully, you will see the following **Test Complete** banner appear in the **Summary** tab of the Recovery Plan:

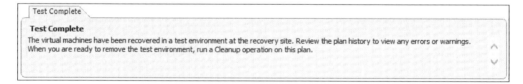

How does a test work?

The testing of a Recovery Plan is done in such a way that it doesn't affect the current operations, which include replication schedules and the actual replicas, or the protected virtual machines. In this section of the chapter, we will learn how this is achieved.

The following figure shows an overview of the steps involved during the testing of a Recovery Plan:

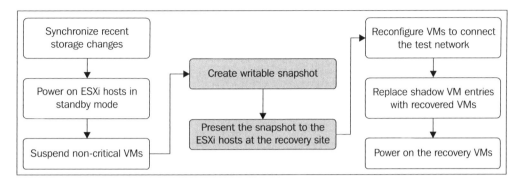

When you initiate a test, SRM instructs the **Storage Replication Adapter** to execute a replication cycle to replicate the latest changes to the replica LUN at the recovery site. However, this will only happen if you had chosen to leave the default option to replicate recent changes checked. You wouldn't need to replicate the recent change when the replication is synchronous, as the replica would already have the latest change. Refer to your replication vendor documentation for more information.

Once the replication is complete, it then needs to find a way to present the replica LUN's data to the recovery ESXi hosts so that the virtual machines can be powered on. This is achieved differently by different storage arrays. The most common methodology is to create a writable snapshot of the replica LUN, and then present the snapshot to the recovery ESXi hosts. The hosts will subsequently scan their HBAs to detect the VMFS volumes on the LUN.

Before the snapshot is presented to the ESXi hosts, SRM needs to make sure that there is enough room (compute capacity) at the recovery site to power on the recovered VMs. To make room for the VMs, SRM could power off the noncritical VMs (*if included in the Recovery Plan*) and also power up the ESXi hosts that were put into the standby mode (if any) by the **Distributed Power Management** (**DPM**).

 The noncritical VMs that SRM chooses to suspend are those that were marked as noncritical for the Recovery Plan, using the **Add Non-Critical VM** option.

To power on the recovered VMs, they have to be registered to the recovery site's vCenter Server. This is achieved by replacing the shadow VM entries with the entries corresponding to the recovered VMs. Keep in mind that the shadow VMs are mere inventory objects and that they do not have any VMDKs mapped to them.

The VMs are then configured to connect to the test network. The test network can either be a port group that you created for the test or an auto bubble network created on a new vSphere Standard Switch with no physical uplinks.

The following screenshot shows a vSphere **Standard Switch** and a **Port Group** that was automatically created during a test for the auto bubble network:

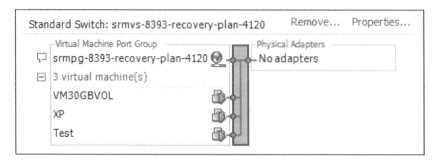

Once the VMs have been configured to connect to the test network, they are powered on. Keep in mind that the testing of a Recovery Plan does not affect the power state of the protected virtual machines at the protected site.

Performing the cleanup after a test

We know from the previous section that during the course of the testing of a Recovery Plan, SRM executes the creation of certain elements to enact a disaster recovery in a manner that will not affect the running environment. Hence, the changes made and the objects created are temporary and have to be cleaned up after a successful test. Fortunately, this is not a manual process either. SRM provides an automated method to perform a cleanup.

The following actions will occur during a cleanup:

- The ESXi hosts will be put back into the DPM standby mode
- The Recovery VMs will be powered off
- The Suspended noncritical VMs will be powered on
- The inventory entries of the Recovery VMs will be replaced with their corresponding Shadow VM entries
- The VMFS volume will be unmounted

- The LUN device will be detached
- The storage initiators and Refresh Storage System will be rescanned
- The writable snapshot that was created will be deleted
- The Port Group and the vSwitch that were created for the bubble network will be removed

The following procedure will guide you through the steps required for the cleanup:

1. Navigate to the vCenter Server's inventory home page and click on **Site Recovery**.
2. Click on **Recovery Plans** on the left pane.
3. Select the Recovery Plan with the status **Test Complete**.
4. Click on the **Cleanup** item in the toolbar, as shown in the following screenshot, to bring up the cleanup wizard:

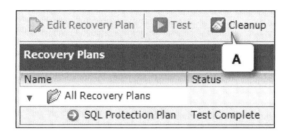

5. In the cleanup wizard, the details regarding the current protected and recovery sites, their connection status, and the number of protected VMs are displayed. Note that the **Force Cleanup** option is grayed out. This option will only be available if the cleanup operation attempt has failed during the previous attempt. Click on **Next** to continue.
6. The next screen will summarize the cleanup options selected. Click on **Start** to initiate the cleanup.
7. The **Recent Tasks** pane should show the **Cleanup Test Recovery** task as successfully completed.

Performing a Planned Migration

VMware SRM can be used to migrate your workload from one site to another. A Planned Migration is done when the protected site is available and is running the virtual machine workload.

There are many use cases, of which the following two are prominent:

- When migrating your infrastructure to a new hardware
- When migrating your virtual machine storage from one array to another

 A Planned Migration will replicate the most recent changes with the help of storage replication. This is not optional.

The following procedure will guide you through the steps required to perform a Planned Migration:

1. Navigate to the vCenter Server's inventory home page and click on **Site Recovery**.

2. Click on **Recovery Plans** on the left pane.

3. Select the Recovery Plan that was created for the Planned Migration and click on the **Recovery** toolbar item, as shown in the following screenshot, to bring up the recovery wizard:

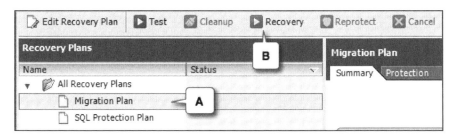

4. As shown in the following screenshot, the first screen will seek a **Recovery Confirmation**. The **Recovery Type** will be preselected as **Planned Migration**. You should acknowledge the recovery confirmation to proceed further. Click on **Next** to continue.

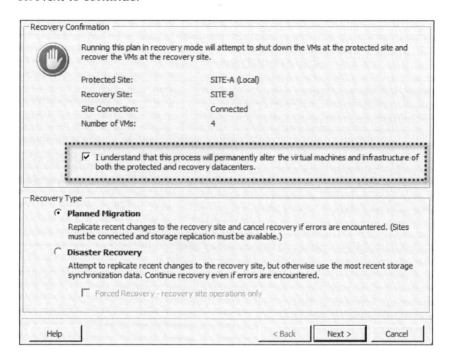

5. The next screen will summarize the wizard options that were selected. Click on **Start** to initiate the migration.

6. The **Recent Tasks** pane should now show the **Failover Recovery Plan** task as successfully completed.

The Planned Migration will not proceed further if any of the recovery steps fail. However, when you re-attempt the Planned Migration, it would resume the operation from the step at which it failed. This enables you to fix the problem and resume from where it failed, saving a considerable amount of time.

The following flowchart shows the logical sequence of events that would occur during the course of a Planned Migration:

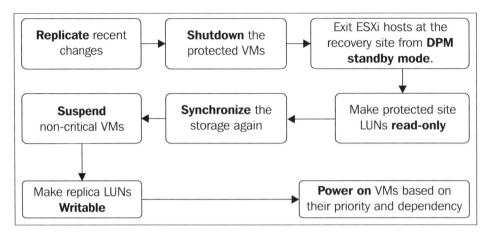

Performing a disaster recovery (Failover)

A Failover is performed when the protected site becomes fully or partially unavailable. We use a Recovery Plan that is already created and tested to perform the Failover. Keep in mind that SRM does not automatically determine the occurrence of a disaster at the protected site; hence, a recovery is always to be manually initiated.

The following steps show how to perform a Failover:

1. Navigate to the vCenter Server's inventory home page and click on **Site Recovery**.

2. Click on **Recovery Plans** on the left pane.

3. Select the Recovery Plan that was created for the disaster recovery and click on the **Recovery** toolbar item to bring up the recovery wizard.

4. In the recovery wizard, as shown in the following screenshot, agree to the **Recovery Confirmation**, set the **Recovery Type** as **Disaster Recovery**, and click on **Next** to continue:

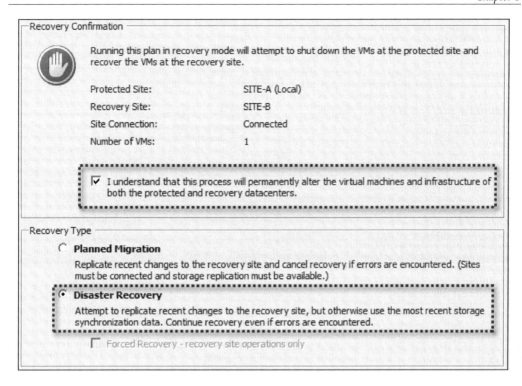

5. The next screen will summarize the selected wizard options. Click on **Start** to perform the recovery.

6. The **Recovery Steps** tab of the Recovery Plan will show the progress of each of the steps involved.

7. Once the Failover is complete, the status of the Recovery Plan should read **Recovery Complete**.

The recovery steps involved in a disaster recovery (Failover) is the same as in that of a Planned Migration, except for the fact that SRM ignores any unsuccessful attempts to pre-synchronize the storage or shut down the protected virtual machines.

Forced Recovery

Forced Recovery is used when the protected site is no longer operational enough to allow SRM to perform its tasks at the protected site before the Failover.

For instance, there is an unexpected power outage at the protected site causing not just the ESXi hosts but also the storage array to become unavailable. In this scenario, SRM cannot perform any of its tasks, such as shutting down the protected VMs or replicating the most recent storage changes (if the replication is asynchronous), at the protected site.

Enabling Forced Recovery for a site

Forced Recovery is not enabled by default, but it can be enabled at the site's advanced settings. To do so, perform the following steps:

1. Navigate to the vCenter Server's inventory home page and click on **Site Recovery**.

2. Click on **Sites** on the left pane.

3. Right-click on the site and click on **Advanced Settings**.

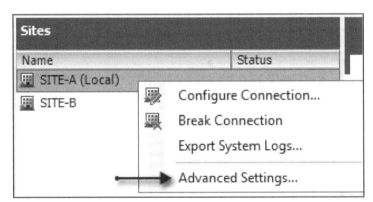

4. In the **Advanced Settings** windows, select the category **recovery** from the left pane.

5. Select the checkbox against the **recovery.forceRecovery** setting, as shown in the following screenshot, and click on **OK** to enable Forced Recovery:

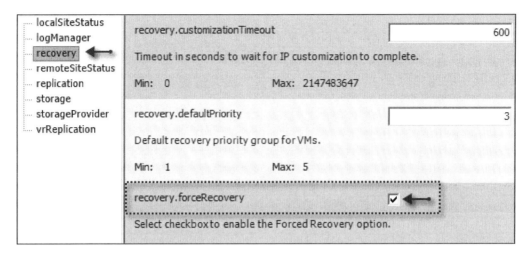

Running Forced Recovery

Running Forced Recovery will skip all the steps that otherwise should have been performed against the protected site. You should use Forced Recovery only during circumstances where the protected site is completely down, leaving no connectivity to either the ESXi hosts or the storage array. If Forced Recovery were to be executed while the protected site is still online and available, then it would leave the virtual machines running at both the protected and recovery sites, causing a split-brain condition for SRM. Furthermore, if the array-based replication was asynchronous, then the chances are that the virtual machines that were started at the recovery site are running old data compared to the ones in the protected site. So, it very important that you take caution before you plan to execute Forced Recovery.

The following steps show how Forced Recovery is executed:

1. Navigate to the vCenter Server's inventory home page and click on **Site Recovery**.
2. Click on **Recovery Plans** on the left pane.
3. Right-click on the Recovery Plan that you want to run and click on **Recovery**.

4. In the recovery wizard, select the **I understand that this process will permanently alter the virtual machines and infrastructure of both the protected and recovery datacenters** checkbox.

5. As shown in the following screenshot, select the **Recovery Type** as **Disaster Recovery**, select the checkbox **Forced Recovery – recovery site operations only**, and click on **Next**:

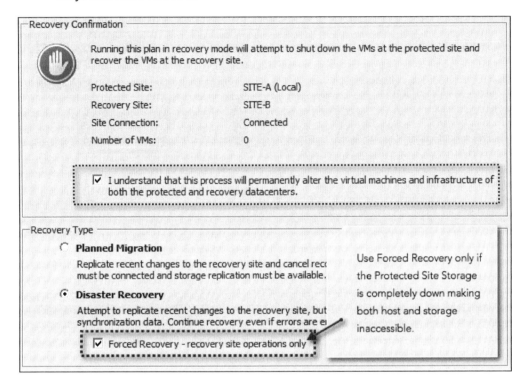

6. You will be prompted to confirm the **Forced Recovery**. Click on **Yes** to confirm.

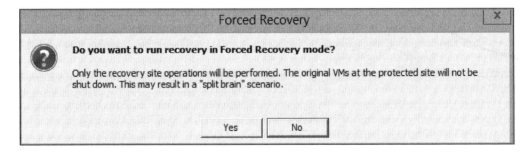

7. Review the operation summary and click on **Start** to initiate the Forced Recovery.

Reprotecting a site

After you Failover the workload from a protected site to the recovery site, the recovery site has no protection enabled for the new workload that it has begun hosting. SRM provides a method to enable protection of the recovery site. This method is called **Reprotect**.

A Reprotect operation will reverse the direction of the replication, thus designating the recovery site as the new protected site. The Reprotect operation can only be done on a Recovery Plan with the **Recovery Complete** status. Also, keep in mind that a Reprotect operation can only be executed when you have repaired the failed site and made it available to become a recovery site.

For instance, let's assume that SITE-A and SITE-B are the protected and recovery sites, respectively. If workload at SITE-A were failed over to SITE-B, then to Reprotect SITE-B, SITE-A should be made accessible. This would mean fixing the problems that caused the failure at SITE-A.

The following steps show how to perform the Reprotect operation:

1. Navigate to the vCenter Server's inventory home page and click on **Site Recovery**.
2. Click on **Recovery Plans** in the left pane.
3. Select the **Recovery Plan** with the **Recovery Complete** status, as shown in the following screenshot, and click on the toolbar item **Reprotect**:

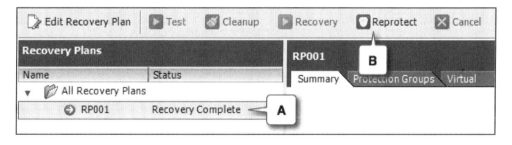

4. In the **Reprotect** wizard screen, agree to the **Reprotect Confirmation** and click on **Next** to continue:

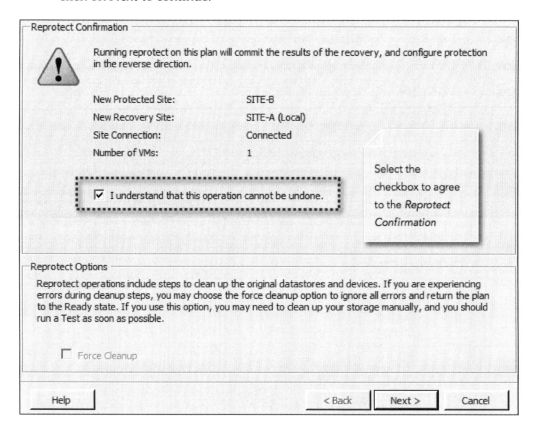

5. In the next screen, click on **Start** to begin the Reprotect operation.

6. You should see a progressing **Reprotect Recovery Plan** task in the **Recent Tasks** pane. Also, the **Recovery Steps** tab will show the progress of every step involved in the Reprotect operation.

7. The status of the Recovery Plan after a successful Reprotect operation should read **Ready**.

Failback to the protected site

In a scenario where, after a Failover, the original protected site is fixed and is made available to host the virtual machine workload, you can use SRM to automate a Failback.

The Failback, although automated, is a two-step process, which is as follows:

- Step 1 will be to perform a Reprotect operation. Read the *Reprotecting a site* section in this chapter to learn how to perform a Reprotect operation.

- Step 2 will be to perform a Failover. Read the *Performing a disaster recovery (Failover)* section in this chapter to learn how to perform a Failover.

Configuring VM recovery properties

The VM recovery properties help in further customizing the recovery procedure at a per-VM level. Although these properties are only available via a Recovery Plan, the changes made to these properties are retained for the VM, regardless of the Recovery Plan they would be included in.

The following are the properties that can be set on a protected virtual machine:

- **IP Settings**
- **Priority Group**
- **VM Dependencies**
- **Shutdown Action**
- **Startup Action**
- **Pre-power On Steps**
- **Post Power On Steps**

Here is how you could get to the **Recovery Properties** of a virtual machine:

1. Navigate to the vCenter Server's inventory home page and click on **Site Recovery**.
2. Click on **Recovery Plans** on the left pane.
3. Select a **Recovery Plan (A)** and navigate to its **Virtual Machines** tab (**B**), which should list all the virtual machines that are included in the Recovery Plan.

4. Select a virtual machine from the list (**C**) and click on **Configure Recovery** (**D**) to bring up the VM recovery properties:

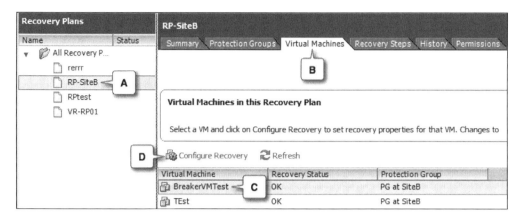

The VM **Properties** windows will show all the properties available for customization. We will visit each of these properties further in this section.

IP settings

The IP settings property is a per-vNIC property for the virtual machine that is part of the Recovery Plan. It is used to customize the IP configuration of the virtual machine during a Planned Migration/Failover.

As the settings are per vNIC, you should enable the IP customization for each of the vNIC that you want to supply the IP settings for. It is done by choosing the vNIC from the left pane (**A**) and then selecting the **Customize IP setting during recovery** checkbox (**B**), as shown in the following screenshot:

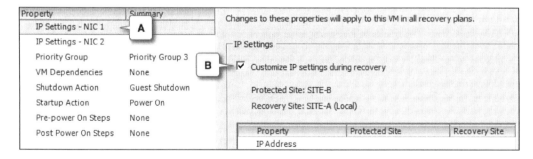

The IP setting can be separate for both the protected and recovery sites.

To configure the IP settings for a Recovery from the original recovery site to the original protected site, use the **Configure Protection** option (**P**), and to configure the IP settings for a Recovery from the protected site to the recovery site, use the **Configure Recovery** option (**R**), as shown in the following screenshot:

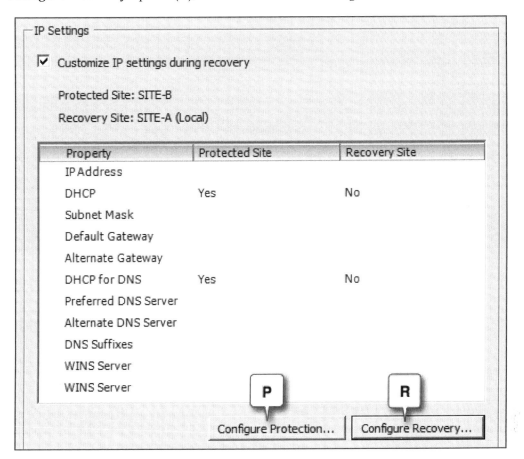

When you hit either **Configure Protection** or **Configure Recovery**, a new IP settings window is shown. You can either choose to use DHCP, IPv4, or IPv6. It also has options to supply the DNS Server details. You could also choose to fetch the current IP configuration of the VM using the **Retrieve** button. For the retrieve operation to work, you need VMware Tools installed and running in the VM:

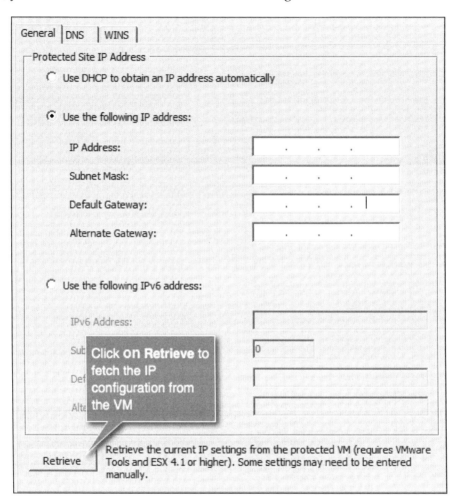

Once the settings have been supplied, click on **OK** to save the IP customization.

Priority Group

Priority Groups are used to set the startup order of the virtual machines. SRM uses five Priority Groups numbered from 1 to 5. Their priority and startup order are shown in the following table:

Priority Group	Priority	Startup order
Priority Group 1	Highest	First
Priority Group 2	Higher than group 3	Before group 3
Priority Group 3	Higher than group 4	Before group 4
Priority Group 4	Higher than group 5	Before group 5
Priority Group 5	Lowest	Last

As shown in the following screenshot, the VMs of the lowest numbered Priority Group are started first:

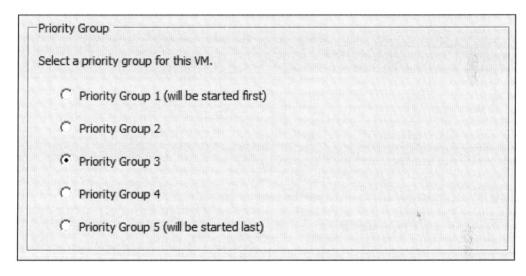

By default, every VM is in **Priority Group 3**. During a Failover, SRM will wait for all the VMs in a **Priority Group** to Failover successfully or fail to Failover before it attempts to power on VMs from a group with lower priority. For instance, SRM will wait for all the VMs in **Priority Group 2** to Failover before it can attempt the Failover of the VMs in **Priority Group 3**. This is because **Priority Group 2** has a higher priority than **Priority Group 3**.

VM Dependencies

So, what happens if all the VMs running the services of the three-tier application are in the same Priority Group? Can we configure a startup order within a Priority Group? The answer is yes. This is where VM Dependencies come in handy.

Let's consider a three-tier application, which has a database, a server component, and the user interface component hosted on three different VMs. Now, in this case the server component is dependent on the availability of the database, and the user interface component is dependent on the server component. This means the database VM should start first, then the VM hosting the service component, and finally the VM hosting the user interface component. Such a startup order can be achieved using the VM Dependencies Recovery Property.

The following steps show how a VM Dependency startup order is created:

1. Get to the Recovery Properties of the virtual machine.

2. Select the **VM Dependencies** property from the left pane (**A**).

3. Click on **Add** to browse and add VMs to the list (**B**). Only the VMs from the Protection Groups that are part of the Recovery Plan can be added as shown in the following screenshot:

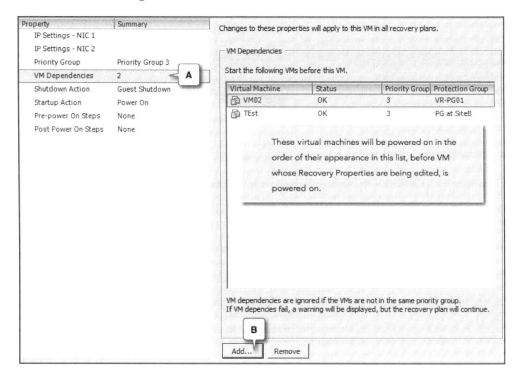

4. Once the virtual machines are added, click on **OK** to save the settings. Keep in mind that the virtual machines are started in the order of their appearance in the list. So make sure that you plan to add the VMs in the order in which you want them to start. You can also remove a VM from the list by hitting the **Remove** button.

 Note that the dependencies between VMs of different Priority Groups are ignored by SRM. Also, the dependencies are not mandatory rules; hence, they wouldn't stop the Recovery Plan from continuing. If a VM dependency fails, it throws a warning and proceeds with the execution of the Recovery Plan.

The Shutdown Action

The Shutdown Action VM Recovery property will let you choose whether a virtual machine at the protected site will be attempted to gracefully shut down or powered off during a Planned Migration or disaster recovery. It also lets you set the amount of time SRM waits on VMware Tools to shut down the virtual machine before it issues a power off. The default timeout value is **5** minutes:

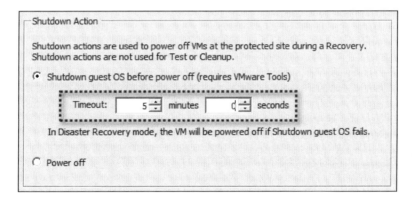

A disaster recovery will power off the VM after the timeout, but a Planned Migration will not proceed further if the VM cannot be gracefully shut down.

The Startup Action

The Startup Action property will let you choose whether or not to power on a virtual machine at the recovery site during a test or a Recovery operation. By default, after a virtual machine is powered on at the recovery site, SRM waits for 5 minutes to determine whether the virtual machine tools have started. If it sees no response from VMware Tools, it marks a failure of that task and proceeds with the Recovery operation. However, the Recovery operation will have an **Incomplete Recovery** status. You can also add further delay before any of the dependent VM are started or before the execution of any **Post Power On Steps**. This is commonly used to give the service running in the VM an additional time to start.

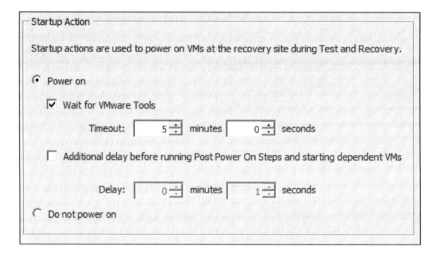

The Pre-power On Steps and Post Power On Steps properties

The **Pre-power On Steps** and **Post Power On Steps** are **VM Recovery Properties** that allow the insertion of additional steps into the Recovery Plan.

With the **Pre-power On Steps** property, you can create the following type of steps:

- A Windows batch command on the SRM Server
- A message prompt, which the user/administrator should dismiss before the Recovery Plan can begin its execution

With the **Post Power On Steps** property, you can create the following type of steps:

- A command on the Recovered virtual machine
- A Windows batch command on the SRM Server

Creating a message prompt is straightforward. It is done in the following way:

1. Select the **Pre-power On Step / Post Power On Step** property from the left plane and click on **Add**.

2. In the **Add Pre-power On Step / Add Post Power On Step** window, select the **Type** as **Prompt (requires a user to dismiss before the plan will continue)**.

3. Supply a **Name** and **Content** and click on **OK** to save the setting.

To create a Windows batch command on the SRM Server, perform the following steps:

1. Select the **Pre-power On Step / Post Power On Steps** property from the left plane and click on **Add**.

2. In the **Add Pre-power On Step / Add Post Power On Step** window, select **Command on SRM Server** as the **Type**.

3. Supply a **Name** of the script and the command script in the **Content** section. Type the actual command. For instance, to run a batch script in `D:\demoscript.bat`, include the following command:

   ```
   c:\windows\system32\cmd.exe /c d:\demoscript.bat
   ```

 For cmd.exe, always mention the absolute path `c:\windows\system32\cmd.exe`

The default timeout for a batch command is 5 minutes. If the batch file doesn't finish executing within 5 minutes, then the execution of the Recovery Plan will stop with an error indicating the same.

Summary

In this chapter, we learned how to use the SRM to orchestrate the testing of a Recovery Plan, performing Planned Migrations and recovery. We also learned how to Failback to a designated protected site after a Failover.

4
Deploying vSphere Replication 5.5

In this chapter, you will learn the following topics:

- New features in vSphere Replication 5.5
- Understanding the vSphere Replication architecture
- Downloading the vSphere Replication bundle
- Deploying the vSphere Replication Appliance
- Setting up the VRA hostname and a VRM site name for the VRA
- Configuring a SQL database for VRMS
- Deploying a vSphere Replication Server
- Registering vSphere Replication Servers

Introduction

Most organizations will have a DR plan in place, regardless of whether it is a large enterprise or a small or medium business. VMware Site Recovery Manager leveraging an array-based replication is a very effective DR solution. However, an array-based replication can be a costly solution for some businesses, especially the small and medium businesses. VMware's proprietary replication engine called vSphere Replication offers a very cost-effective DR solution without the need for investments on storage replication technologies.

One of the advantages for businesses using vSphere Replication is the fact that the replication can be managed without the need for an SRM license. The vSphere Web Client GUI provides an interface to configure and manage replication on virtual machines.

In this chapter, we learn what vSphere Replication actually is, its architecture, and how it can be deployed in your vSphere environment.

vSphere Replication is a replication engine that can be leveraged to configure replication on individual virtual machines. It can replicate a virtual machine and its disks from one location to another without the need to incorporate an expensive array-based replication. What it really does is provide a mechanism to replicate a virtual machine using the existing Ethernet infrastructure and recover them when there is a need.

The concept of vSphere Replication was introduced with VMware Site Recovery Manager Version 5.0. At that time, vSphere Replication was not a standalone product. vSphere v5.1 onwards, vSphere Replication became a standalone product and directly integrates into the vSphere platform. It registers itself as a plugin to the vCenter Server. All of the replication and recovery operations are done using the vSphere Web Client. It is included in Essentials Plus and higher license models.

It is storage agnostic, which means that a virtual machine or its disk files can be replicated to a datastore, regardless of it being a VMFS volume or an NFS mount. For instance, if the virtual machine that you want to protect by enabling replication is located on a VMFS volume, then the replica can be either on another VMFS volume or an NFS mount. This stands true both ways.

 vSphere Replication can protect a maximum of 500 virtual machines.

VMware Site Recovery Manager can be configured to leverage the vSphere Replication engine to perform recovery tests, Failovers, Planned Migration, Failback, and so on.

New features of vSphere Replication 5.5

vSphere Replication was greatly improved with the release of the Version 5.5. Some of the new features and improvements are explored in the following sections.

Multiple points-in-time replication snapshots (historical retention)

You can now have multiple points-in-time snapshots (a maximum of 24 snapshots) of your replicated data. The number of snapshots and the retention period can be specified when configuring replication for a virtual machine.

Multiple vSphere Replication Server appliances per vCenter

With vSphere 5.5, you can now deploy up to 10 vSphere Replication Server appliances per vCenter in a standalone mode.

 Keep in mind that a **vSphere Replication Server (VR Server)** is not a **vSphere Replication Appliance (VRA)**. We will discuss more about the differences in the architecture section.

By standalone mode, we mean that the replication is managed without the use of **Site Recovery Manager (SRM)**. Prior to Version 5.5, the number of VR appliances that can be deployed in the standalone mode were limited to only one and with SRM, it was 10. Deploying multiple VRs can have several use cases. It is not mandatory to have a vCenter at a datacenter to deploy a VR appliance.

A VR appliance can simply be deployed at a remote datacenter to handle the replication traffic sent to it and the writing of the data onto a chosen datastore at that site. This new ability drives several use cases. For instance, if you were to maintain a remote datacenter only to hold replicated data, then you don't necessarily have to deploy a vCenter Server at that site. You can manage the datacenter with an existing vCenter Server, and a VR appliance deployed on one of ESXi hosts at the remote site should do the job of collating the replication traffic and writing it onto the intended datastore.

Storage vMotion of protected VMs

You now perform storage vMotion of a replicated, protected VM to any datastore. However, this can only be done with VMs at a protected site and not with the replicas at the recovery site. The replicas are not registered to any of the ESXi hosts at the target site.

Storage profiles and vSAN compatibility

VM storage profiles can now be used to with vSphere Replication. You can also now use vSphere Replication with vSAN, but there are several caveats. However, vSAN itself is an experimental feature with vSphere 5.5.

For more information regarding the use of vSphere Replication with vSAN, refer to page 51 of the vSphere Replication Administration guide at `http://bit.ly/VRAdminGuide`.

Performance improvement

VMware claims that the replication is now faster. It uses a new TCP stack optimization for latency handling. The following are the two aspects:

- It implements buffered I/O for improved NFC write performance

- Disk blocks sent across are coalesced or aggregated, and it is only then the disk is opened for the WRITE operation to be performed

 There are several other improvements. For more information, read the What's New section of the vSphere Replication 5.5 Release Notes at http://bit.ly/VR_WhatIsNew.

This performance improvement, however, does not affect the stated RPO (which should be greater or equal to 15 minutes and less than or equal to 24 hours) for vSphere Replication. The performance improvement is for the data transfer and handling. This means it can now handle more replications, hence more data.

Understanding the vSphere Replication architecture

vSphere Replication is VMware's hypervisor-based replication solution. Unlike the array-based replication, the data is replicated over the network using the VMware **Network File Copy** (**NFC**) protocol. VMware NFC is a proprietary VMware protocol that is used to transfer disk (VMDK) blocks between ESXi hosts.

The vSphere Replication architecture involves the following components:

- One or more instances of vCenter Servers managing the protected and the recovery sites

- A **vSphere Replication Appliance** (**VRA**) deployed at the protected site

- A VRA or a vSphere Replication Server at the recovery site

- The VRM plugin for the vSphere Web Client

- The vSphere Replication agent that runs on every ESXi host

A vSphere Replication Appliance is a vApp comprising of the **vSphere Replication Management Server** (**VRMS**) and a VR Server. For vSphere Replication to work, you will need a VRMS at the protected site and a VR Server at the target recovery site, be it local or remote; and there can be only one VRMS per vCenter Server. Refer to the following diagram:

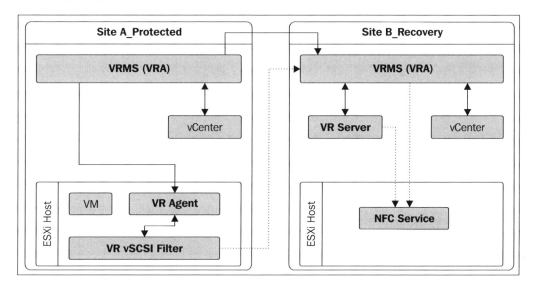

The recovery site is where you plan to maintain the replicas of the virtual machines from the protected site. It is the site to which you will be sending the replication traffic. The vSphere Replication Appliances provides a replication management interface via the vSphere Web Client. It registers itself as a plugin for the vSphere Web Client.

Every ESXi host starting with Version 5.1 has a vSphere Replication agent already built into the VMkernel, thereby removing the dependency on Site Recovery Manager and installing additional packages into each ESXi host.

Downloading the vSphere Replication bundle

The vSphere Replication Server appliance is available for download as an ISO data file or a compressed ZIP package, both of which contain separate OVFs for vSphere Replication Appliance and add-on servers.

The **vSphere Replication Appliance (VRA)** includes a vSphere Replication Management Server and a vSphere Replication Server. It includes a plugin for the vSphere Web Client and also uses a vPostgreSQL embedded database.

To download the ISO or ZIP bundle, use the following steps:

1. Go to the vSphere downloads page at `www.vmware.com/go/download-vsphere`.
2. Click on the **Go to Downloads** hyperlink corresponding to **vSphere Replication 5.5** listed under your license model.
3. Log in to your **My VMware** account when prompted.
4. Download either the ZIP or ISO package.

Deploying the vSphere Replication Appliance

The vSphere Replication Appliance should be installed at a site where you have virtual machines that need to be protected. It may or may not be required to be installed on both the protected and recovery sites. You will need VRA to be deployed at the recovery site only if you intend to pair it with the protected site. Refer to the following diagram:

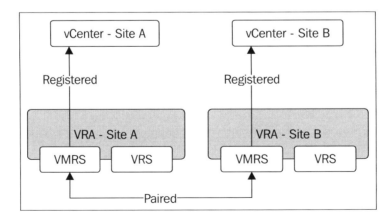

The pairing is done by adding the recovery site as a target site to the VRMS at the protected site. Read the *Adding a remote site as a target* section in *Chapter 5, Configuring and Using vSphere Replication 5.5*, for information on how to achieve this.

The total number of the virtual machines that can be protected by vSphere Replication is 500 per site. The limit is per VRMS, and as there can be only one VRMS registered to a site's vCenter, the 500 VM limit cannot be exceeded. If the VRMSs are paired, then the cumulative limit of VMs from both the sites becomes 500 and not 1000. To deploy the vSphere Replication Appliances, you need the following components:

- vCenter 5.5
- ESXi hosts compatible with Version 5.5 of vCenter Server
- The downloaded bundle for vSphere Replication 5.5

The appliance's OVF can be deployed using the **Deploy OVF Template** wizard. The wizard can be initiated from various levels (vCenter or datacenter or ESXi). We will do it at the vCenter level, which however is not a technical requirement. Refer to the following steps:

1. Extract (unzip) the downloaded package, or in case you have downloaded the ISO bundle, then mount the ISO to the vCenter Server virtual machine or the machine on which the vSphere Client is being accessed from.

2. Right-click on the **vCenter Server** and click on **Deploy OVF Template**. Refer to the following screenshot:

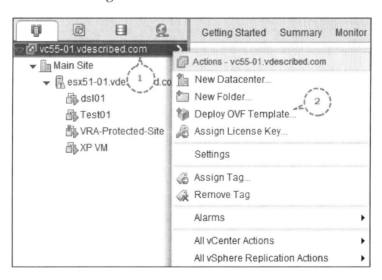

3. On the wizard screen, set the source as **Local file** and click on **Browse**, as shown in the following screenshot:

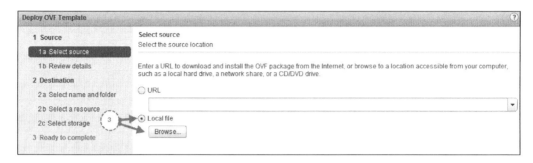

4. Navigate to the extracted bundle folder and then to the `bin` subfolder, as shown in the following screenshot:

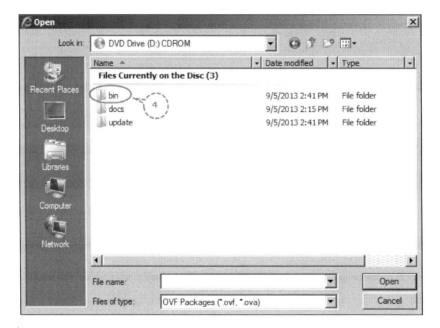

5. Select the OVF file `vSphere_Replication_OVF10.ovf` and click on **Open** to make the selection and return to the wizard. Refer to the following screenshot:

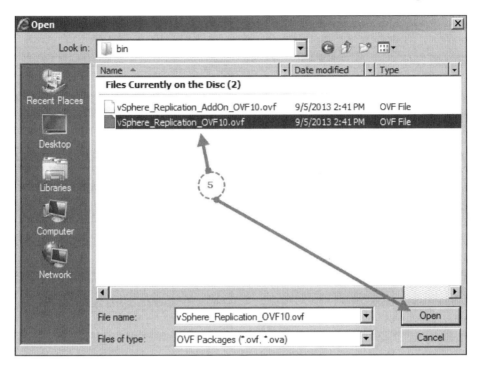

6. On the wizard screen, click on **Next** to continue.

7. The **Review details** screen summarizes the appliance's details. Click on **Next** to continue.

8. On the **License Agreement** screen, select **Accept** to receive the license and click on **Next** to continue.

9. Provide a name for the VM, select an inventory destination for it, and click on **Next** to continue, as shown in the following screenshot:

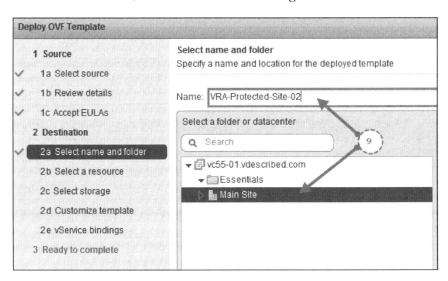

10. Select a compute location for the VM. The compute location could be an ESXi host or a cluster of ESXi hosts. Once a selection has been made, click on **Next** to continue. Refer to the following screenshot:

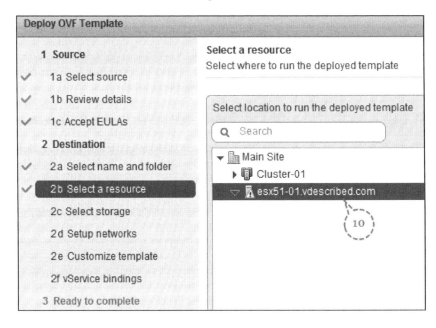

11. Select the VMDK type and a datastore for the VM and click on **Next** to continue, as shown in the following screenshot:

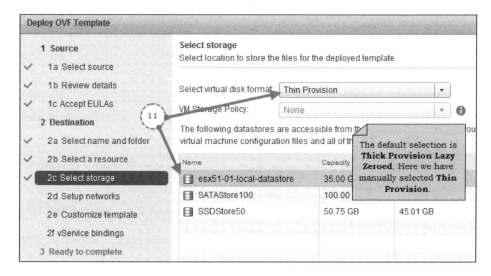

12. Select a network (port group) for the VM's vNIC, and choose between IPv4 or IPv6, and an IP allocation policy (DHCP/Static). We have selected **Static**, hence we will have to manually specify the DNS Server, the Subnet Mask, and the gateway of the subnet the VM will be a part of. Once done, click on **Next** to continue. Refer the following screenshot:

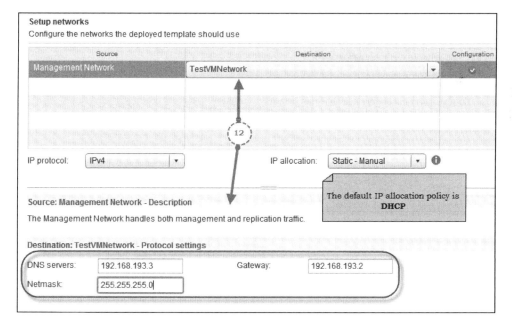

13. Set the password and the static IP for the appliance as shown in the following screenshot. Click on **Next** to continue.

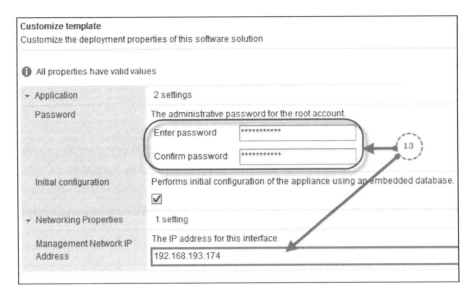

14. The next screen will show the vService binding details. There is nothing to modify here, so click on **Next** to continue.

15. On the **Ready to complete** screen, review the settings and then click on **Finish** to deploy the appliance VM. You can select the **Power on after deployment** checkbox to start the VM if the deployment is successful.

How does it work?

Once deployed, the appliance will power on and finish the initial configuration, which includes the configuration of the embedded database and the process of registering VRMS to the vCenter Server.

You can only have a single instance of VRMS registered to a vCenter Server. This means that you can't deploy multiple instances of vSphere Replication Appliance at a site. If you do so, then the appliance will detect that there is another appliance that has already been registered to the vCenter Server and will prompt for an override or a shutdown of the newly deployed appliance. The following screenshot shows an appliance initialization detecting the presence of another VRA:

```
┌───────────────────vSphere Replication────────────────────┐
│  Another vSphere Replication Appliance (192.168.193.170)  │
│  is already registered with the vCenter Server.           │
│                                                           │
│  If you choose to continue existing replications will be  │
│  stopped and will need to be configured again with the    │
│  new appliance.                                           │
│                                                           │
│ ───────────────────────────────────────────────────────── │
│          <Continue>              <Shutdown>               │
└───────────────────────────────────────────────────────────┘
```

 If you choose the **Continue** option, you should shut down the already registered VR appliance.

You can, however, deploy multiple instances of the vSphere Replication Server (add-on) server appliance, which doesn't initialize the VRMS component. The add-on server appliance is deployed using a different OVF.

Like with any VMware appliance, the VRS Appliance also has a web-based management interface that can be accessed for appliance-specific configuration tasks. This web interface is called **Virtual Appliance Management Interface** (**VAMI**).

You can use the IP address of the appliance to connect to its management web interface using the URL format: `https://<IP address or FQDN>:5480`.

When you reach the login page for the appliance, log in using the root user and the password you set during the OVF deployment wizard. Once you are in, you will see a **Getting Started** tab, which is a subtab under the **VR** tab. There is nothing much you can do at the **Getting Started** tab. The other subtabs that are available under VR are **Configuration**, **Security**, and **Support**. We do not need to review or change the options under these subtabs unless necessary.

The other main tabs available are **Network**, **Update**, and **System**. These will be covered in the later sections of the chapter, which would require accessing these tabs.

Setting up the VRA hostname and a VRM site name for the VRA

Although not mandatory, you might need to set a hostname and a target name for the vSphere Replication Appliance that you have deployed.

The VRA hostname

The hostname for the appliance can be set from the appliance's VAMI. The default hostname post deployment will be `localhost.localdom`. This can, however, be modified.

The following procedure will guide you through the steps required to modify the hostname:

1. Connect to the VAMI of the appliance. Enter `https://<IP address or FQDN>:5480` as the URL.

2. Log in using the root user and the password that was supplied during the OVF deployment wizard.

3. Navigate to the **Address** tab in the **Network** menu.

 Prior to providing the hostname, it is important to create a new host (*A*) record at the DNS Server. Only then will you be able to connect to the appliance using its hostname.

4. Provide a **Hostname** at the input box corresponding to it and click on **Save Settings**, as shown in the following screenshot:

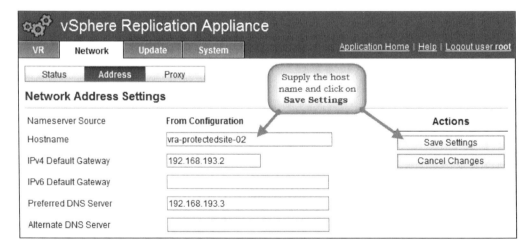

The VRM site name

Every VRM Server registered to a vCenter Server will have a site name. By default, during the initial configuration of the appliance, the address of the vCenter Server to which the VRMS gets registered to is set as the VRM site name. The site name is only a display name; hence, it is not mandatory that you change it. For instance, the VRM site name of a VRMS registered to the protected site vCenter Server can be just called "Protected Site".

The following procedure will guide you through the steps required to modify the VRM site name:

1. Connect to the VAMI of the appliance by entering `https://<IP address or FQDN>:5480` as the URL.

2. Log in using the root user and the password that was supplied during the OVF deployment wizard.

3. Navigate to the **Configuration** tab under the **VR** option.

4. Modify **VRM Site Name** using the input box corresponding to it and restart the VRM Service by clicking on **Save and Restart Service**, as shown in the following screenshot:

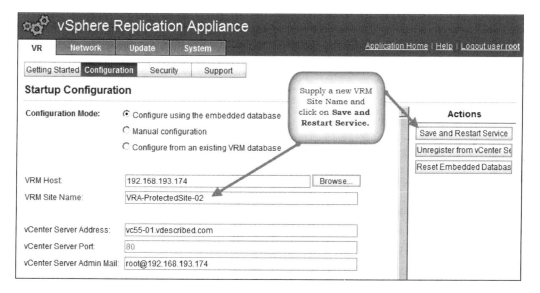

 Sometimes, it can take a while for the appliance to save the setting and restart the VRM service.

Configuring a SQL database for VRMS

The vSphere Replication Appliance, by default, initializes the default embedded vPostgreSQL database. All of the initial configuration data and the replication configuration data will be stored in the embedded database. Therefore, it is important that you plan on the type of database before you configure replication for the VMs. This is because if you were to reconfigure the VRMS component to use an external database, then you will lose the existing replication configuration information. You will need to reconfigure the replication on the VMs. Backup and restoration of an external database is easier because you will have to only back up the database files. If you were to plan a backup of the embedded database, then you will have to back up the entire appliance.

To know which versions of SQL Server are supported, use the **Solution/Database Interoperability** filter on the **VMware Product Interoperability Matrixes** web portal. The portal can be reached by going to **VMware Compatibility Guides** via `http://www.vmware.com/in/guides.html` and clicking on the **Product Interoperability Matrixes** hyperlink.

At the VMware Product Interoperability Matrixes web portal, select **Solution/Database Interoperability** and select **VMware vSphere Replication** as the VMware Product and **5.5** as the **Version**. You can then choose a database from the list and verify its compatibility. Refer to the following screenshot:

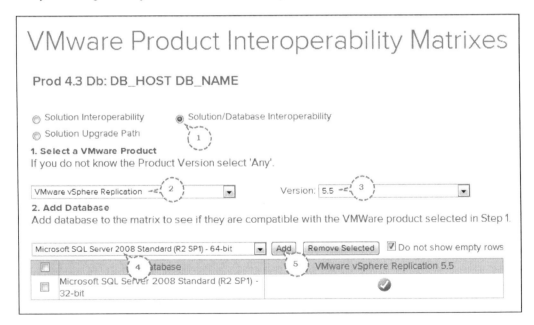

The following procedure will guide you through the steps required to configure a SQL database for the VRMS:

1. Log in to your database server and start **Microsoft SQL Server Management Studio**.

2. From the **Object Explorer** window, right-click on **Database**, and click on **New Database**, as shown in the following screenshot:

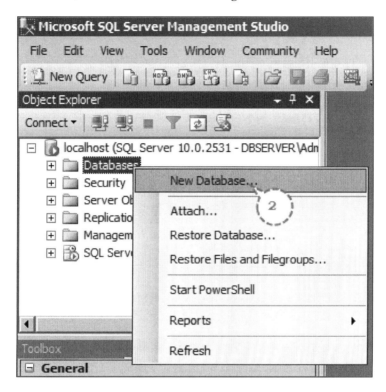

3. In the **New Database** window, provide a **Database name** and leave the rest of the attributes at their defaults for now, and click on **OK**. Refer to the following screenshot:

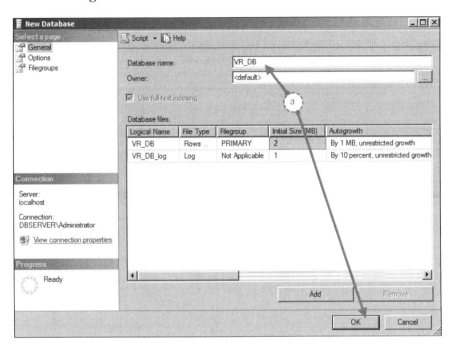

4. From the **Object Explorer** window, expand **Security**, right-click on **Logins**, and click on **New Login**, as shown in the following screenshot:

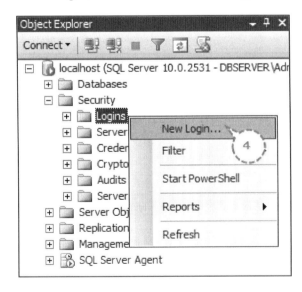

5. In the **Login-New** window, select **SQL Server authentication** and provide a **Login name**, set the password, and deselect **Enforce password policy**, which will void the other two password policies (**User must change password at the next login** and **Enforce password expiration**) as well.

6. Set **Default database** to the newly created DB for vSphere Replication, and click on **OK**. Refer to the following screenshot:

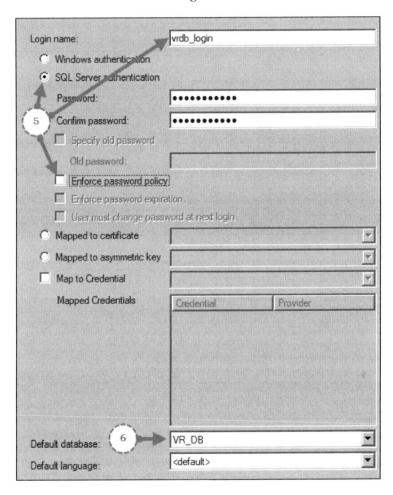

 In this example, we created a DB named VR_DB, so we should be changing the default database to VR_DB.

7. From the **Object Explorer** window, expand **Databases**, right-click on
the new database (VR_DB), and click on **Properties**, as shown in the
following screenshot:

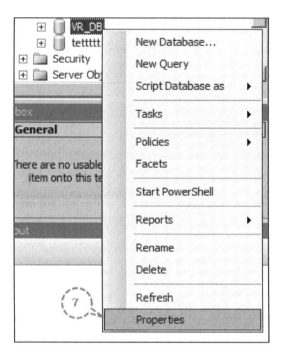

8. In the **Database properties** window, select the **Files** page and
change the database **Owner** to the login you created, as shown
in the following screenshot:

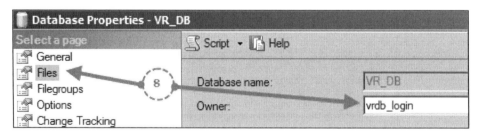

9. From the same window, select the **Options** page, and change **Recovery model** to **Simple**. Refer to the following screenshot:

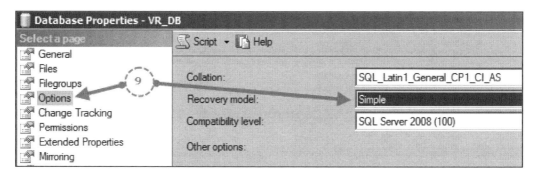

10. Click on **OK** to close the **Database Properties** window.

11. Now, connect to the VAMI of the vSphere Replication Appliance by entering the URL `https://<IP address or FQDN>:5480`.

12. Log in using the root user and the password.

13. Navigate to the **Configuration** tab under the **VR** menu.

14. Set **Configuration Mode** to **Manual configuration**.

15. Set **DB Type** to **SQL Server**.

16. Provide the **DB Host**, which could be the address (FQDN/IP) of the DB Server.

17. Specify **DB Username**, **DB Password**, and **DB Name** as shown in the following screenshot:

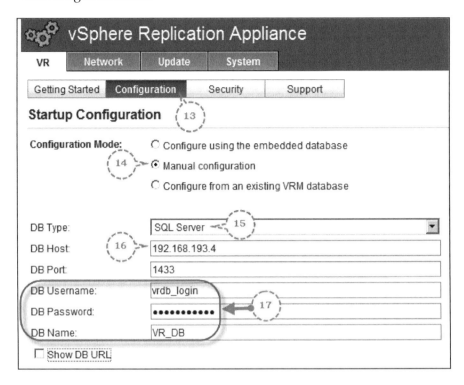

18. Click on **Save and Restart Service**.

Hitting **Save and Restart** will save the new settings and restart the vSphere Replication Management Service. It might take some time to finish, owing to the time it needs to prepare the database. Once done, you will have to reconfigure replications on the VM.

Deploying a vSphere Replication Server

Unlike with the vSphere Replication Appliances, you can deploy additional vSphere Replication Servers using an add-on appliance available in the vSphere Replication deployment bundle that was downloaded. You can deploy up to 10 VR Servers appliances per vCenter Server instance. There are several use cases to deploy additional VR Servers. One of the prime reasons is the manual load distribution. Each VR Server with the default memory configuration of 512 MB can handle up to 100 replications. If there are more than 100 VMs being replicated, then you could either choose to increase the memory of the appliance or deploy additional appliances and load balance by distributing the replication traffic to different appliances.

The following procedure will guide you through the steps required to deploy additional VR Servers:

1. From the vSphere Web Client's home page, click on **vSphere Replication** to bring up the vSphere Web Client's interface for vSphere Replication, as shown in the following screenshot:

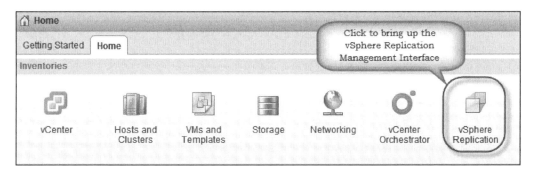

2. This page will list the vCenter Server the VRMS is registered to. Click on the toolbar item **Manage**, which should bring up the **Manage** tab for that vCenter Server with the **vSphere Replication** subtab selected. Refer to the following screenshot:

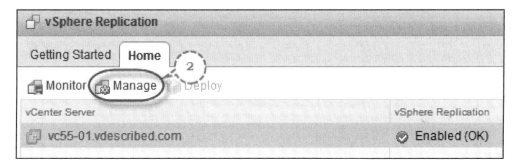

3. Select **Replication Servers**, which is on the left-hand side pane, to view a list of registered VR Servers.

4. Navigate to **Actions** | **All vSphere Replication Actions** | **Deploy VR server** to bring up the **Deploy OVF Template** wizard, as shown in the following screenshot:

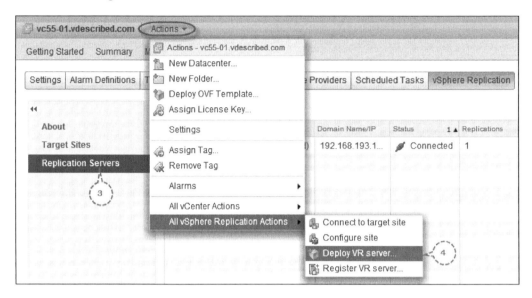

5. Set the source as **Local file** and click on **Browse**.

6. Navigate to the vSphere replication bundle folder and then to the bin subfolder. Select OVF vSphere_Replication_AddOn_OVF10.ovf and click on **Open** to return to the wizard screen.

7. Click on **Next** to continue.

8. The **Review details** screen will summarize the OVF template details. Note that the description says **Additional vSphere Replication Server**. Click on **Next** to continue. Refer to the following screenshot:

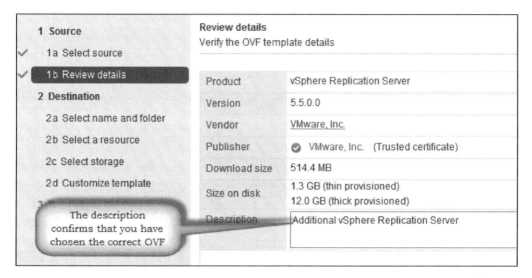

9. Provide a name and inventory location of the VM appliance and click on **Next** to continue.

10. Accept the license agreement and click on **Next**.

11. Provide a name for the VM and select a compute location. The compute location can be either a cluster of ESXi hosts or a single ESXi host. Click on **Next** to continue.

12. Set an intended disk format for the appliance's VMDKs and choose a datastore to store the VM files. The default option is **Thick Provisioned Lazy Zeroed**. Click on **Next** to continue.

13. Select a network (port group) for the VM's vNIC, choose between IPv4 or IPv6, and an IP allocation policy (**DHCP/Static**). Here, we have selected **Static**. Hence, it will have to manually specify the DNS Server, the Subnet Mask, and the gateway the subnet the VM will be part of. Click on **Next** to continue.

14. Set the password and the static IP for the appliance. Click on **Next** to continue.

15. On the **Ready to complete** screen, review the settings and click on **Finish** to deploy the appliance VM. You can select the checkbox **Power on after deployment** to start the VM if the deployment is successful.

Once the VRS is deployed, you will have to register the vSphere Replication Server to the VRMS. For instructions on how to do this, read the following section.

Registering vSphere Replication Servers

The deployed vSphere Replication Servers should be registered to the VRMS for them to be used to handle replication traffic. For instructions on how to deploy vSphere Replication Servers, read the *Deploying a vSphere Replication Server* section in this chapter.

The following procedure will guide you through the steps required to register the vSphere Replication Servers:

1. From the vSphere Web Client's home page, click on **vSphere Replication** to bring up the vSphere Web Client's interface for vSphere Replication.

2. This page will list the vCenter Server the VRMS is registered to. Click on the toolbar item **Manage**, which should bring up the **Manage** tab for that vCenter Server with the **vSphere Replication** subtab selected.

3. Select **Replication Servers**, which is on the left-hand side pane, to view a list of registered VR Servers.

4. Navigate to **Actions | All vSphere Replication Actions | Register VR server**, to bring up the **Register vSphere Replication Server** window. Refer to the following screenshot:

5. Browse through the vCenter inventory to locate the newly deployed VR appliance VM.

6. Click on the **Virtual Machine** to highlight and click on **OK** to confirm the selection, as shown in the following screenshot:

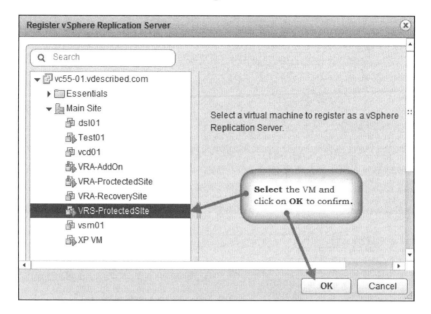

7. Once the registration is successful, it should be listed in the **Replication Servers** page as shown in the following screenshot:

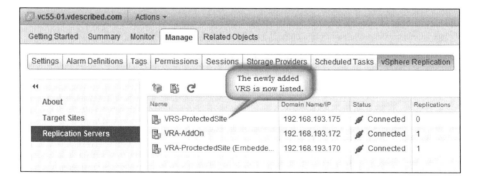

Summary

In this chapter, we learned how to deploy and prepare a vSphere Replication environment. In the next chapter, we will learn how to replicate and recover virtual machines.

5
Configuring and Using vSphere Replication 5.5

In the previous chapter, we learned how to deploy the components required to form a vSphere Replication environment. Now, it is time to take the discussion further. In this chapter, we learn how replication actually works and which configuration tasks are involved with the replication of a virtual machine.

We will be covering the following topics:

- Adding a remote site as a target
- Configuring the replication of a VM to the local site
- Configuring the replication of a VM to the remote site
- How does replication work?
- Using the replication seeds
- Monitoring a replication
- Reconfiguring a replication
- Changing the target datastore
- Pausing an ongoing replication
- Synchronizing data immediately
- Stopping a replication for a VM
- Moving a replication to another VR Server
- Recovering virtual machines
- Configuring a Failback for virtual machines
- Configuring SRM to leverage vSphere Replication

Adding a remote site as a target

A remote vCenter Server can be added as one of the targets. The pairing is mandatory when both the sites are managed by different vCenter Servers. This is because the VRM Server registered to the protected site vCenter can only see VR Servers that are registered to it. You can deploy multiple VR Servers at either of the sites, but it can only be used if they are registered to its local VRM Server. The pairing will not be possible if the vCenter Server managing the remote site does not have a VRMS registered to it. Refer to the following diagram:

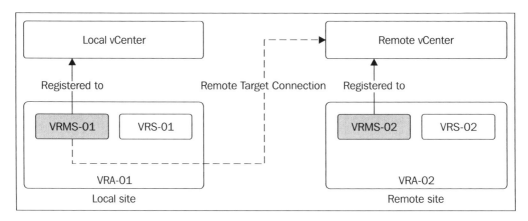

When adding a target site, you are prompted to specify the address (FQDN/IP) and connection credentials of the vCenter Server managing the target site. Most environments use separate accounts for connections between different vSphere components. The separate account could also be a service account corresponding to that component. In this case, you could use the service account corresponding to the vCenter Server that you are adding as a target site. Here, the vCenter Server acts as a proxy to communicate with the VRM Server registered to the target site. Once the connection is successfully made, the VRM Server will be listed as the target site.

The default name of the site of the VRM Server is the name of the vCenter Server it is registered to. This can be changed at the VRA's web interface, under the **Configuration** tab.

The following procedure will guide you through the steps required to add a target site:

1. From the vSphere Web Client's home page, click on **vSphere Replication** to bring up the vSphere Web Client's interface for vSphere Replication, as shown in the following screenshot:

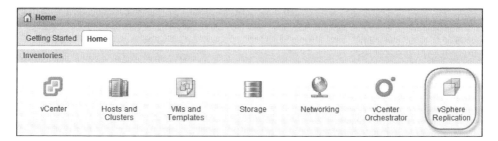

2. This page will list the vCenter Server to which the VRMS Server is registered. Click on the toolbar item **Manage**, which should bring up the **Manage** tab for that vCenter Server with the **vSphere Replication** subtab selected.

3. Click on **Target Site**, which is on the left pane, to list all the current target sites.

4. Navigate to **Actions | All vSphere Replication Actions | Connect to target site** to bring up the **Connect to target site** window, as shown in the following screenshot:

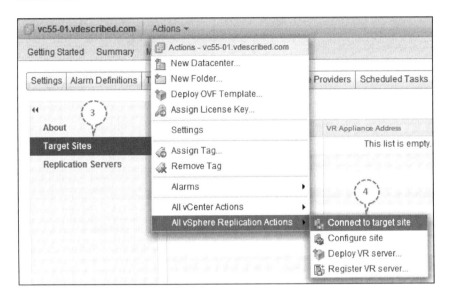

5. Provide the address (FQDN/IP) of the vCenter Server managing the target site and its connection credentials and click on **OK**. Although the following screenshot shows the use of the Administrator account, it is recommended to use a separate account:

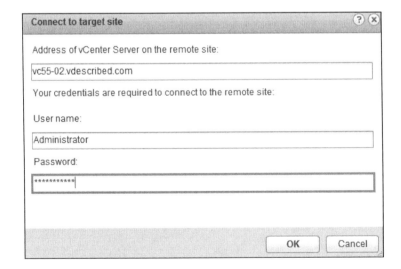

6. Once done, the VRM Server registered to the added vCenter should be listed as the target site.

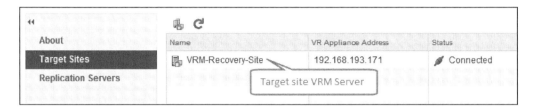

Configuring the replication of a VM to the local site

Replication can be across sites or to the same site. If you choose to replicate the virtual machines that you plan to protect to a datastore at the same site, then you could use vSphere Replication to achieve the same.

Configuring replication requires the availability of a replication server (VRS) at the target site. As you have already deployed a vSphere Replication Appliance that includes both the VRMS and VRS components, there is no need for an additional step to get the replication working at the local site.

The following procedure will guide you through the steps required to configure replication for a VM:

1. Right-click on the virtual machine from the inventory and navigate to the **Configure Replication** tab in **All vSphere Replication Actions**, as shown in the following screenshot:

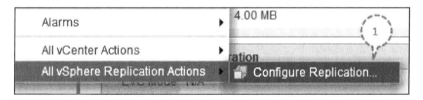

2. Select the local site as the target site and click on **Next**.

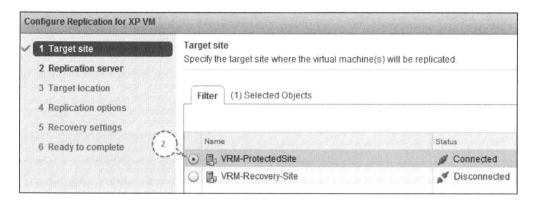

3. You will now have an option to manually select a VR Server to pass the replication traffic through or let VRMS do the selection. Highlight the VR Server that you want to use and click on **Next**.

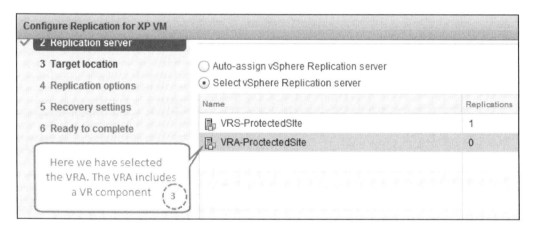

4. Select a datastore where you would like to place the replica of the virtual machine. Optionally, select the checkbox of the **Advanced disk configuration** option and then click on **Next**.

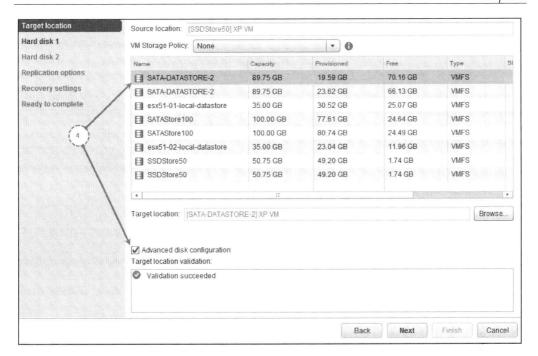

5. Select the virtual disk format and click on **Next** to continue.

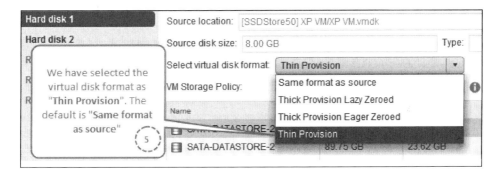

 You will be prompted to make a choice for every VMDK associated with the VM being configured for replication.

6. Choose a guest OS-quiescing method. Currently, the only available quiescing method is Microsoft VSS.

7. Set a planned **Recovery Point Objective (RPO)** value. The default is **4** hours, the lowest possible being **15** minutes and the highest **24** hours. You can also choose a save point for the snapshots of the replication by selecting the checkbox to enable it. By default, it creates **3** points in time instances, and such instances that are created during the last **5** days are retained. You can only retain a maximum of **24** points in time snapshots of the replication. Point in time snapshots are useful if you want to maintain multiple recoverable points for the virtual machine. Make a selection and click on **Next** to continue. Refer to the following screenshot:

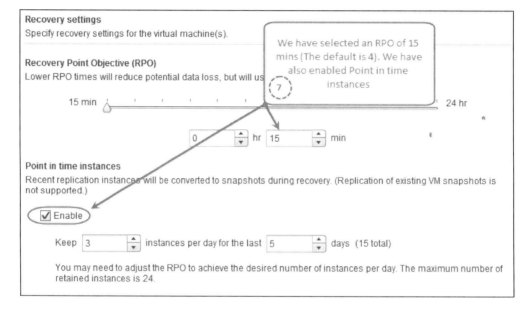

8. On the **Ready to complete** screen, review the settings and click on **Finish** to configure the replication.

9. The **Recent Tasks** pane should show a task **Configure a virtual machine for replication** as completed successfully.

Configuring the replication of a VM to a remote site

You can configure the replication of a VM to a datastore accessible to a remote site. To achieve this, you will need a vSphere Replication Server component at the remote site. For the remote site to be accessible, you will need to add that server as a target site. Read the *Adding a remote site as a target* section in this chapter for more information.

The following procedure will guide you through the steps required to configure the replication of a VM onto a remote site:

1. Add a remote site vCenter as the target site. Read the *Adding a remote site as a target* section in this chapter for instructions.

2. Right-click on the virtual machine from the inventory and navigate to the **Configure Replication** tab in **All vSphere Replication Actions**.

3. Select the remote target site and click on **Next**.

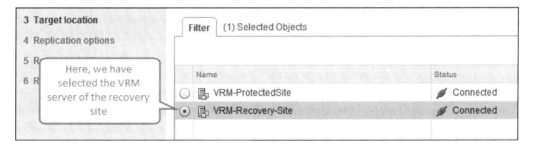

4. You will now have an option to manually select a VR Server to pass the replication traffic through or let VRMS do the selection. Make a selection and click on **Next**.

5. Select a datastore if you like to place the replica of the virtual machine.

6. Select the **Advanced disk configuration** checkbox and click on **Next**.

7. Select the virtual disk format and click on **Next** to continue. You will be prompted to make a choice for every VMDK associated with the VM being configured for replication.

8. Choose a guest OS-quiescing method. Currently the only available quiescing method is Microsoft VSS.

9. Set a planned RPO value. The default is 4 hours, the lowest possible being 15 minutes and the highest 24 hours.

10. You can also choose a save point in snapshots of the replication by selecting the checkbox to enable it. By default, it creates three points in time instances, and such instances created during the last five days are retained. You can only retain a maximum of 24 points in time snapshots of the replication. Make an intended section and click on **Next** to continue.

11. On the **Ready to complete** screen, review the settings and click on **Finish** to configure the replication.

12. The **Recent Tasks** pane should show a task **Configure a virtual machine for replication** as completed successfully.

Regardless of whether a VM is configured to replicate to a local or remote site, the replication works in the same manner. Read the following section for more insight.

How does replication work?

On successfully configuring the replication on a VM, it first does an initial full sync of the source VMDKs to the target datastore. If you already have the base VMDKs previously copied to the destination datastore, then only the changed blocks are replicated. The replication happens over the network using the **Network File Copy (NFC)** protocol. The changed blocks are transferred using ESXi's management VMkernel port group.

Once the initial sync is complete, the VR agent tracks the changed blocks using the vSCSI filter driver. It tracks, writes, and maintains a bitmap of the changed blocks. Every time a replica is created, the data transferred is copied to a redo logfile. This is done to make sure that the VM at the recovery site is not corrupted in the event of a network disruption. The redo log is committed to the base disk only after the changed blocks are fully copied, thereby making each replica crash consistent. When you configure the replication for the VM, you get to choose the RPO and the number of multiple points in time snapshots that you would like to maintain. The RPO ranges from 15 minutes to 24 hours, and you can have up to 24 points in time snapshots. This means you can have up to 24 historical point-time recovery points of the replicated VM.

Both RPO and the number of points in time instances dictate the number of historical snapshots maintained for the VM. For instance, if you set an RPO of 2 hours, then you will retain 12 point-in-time recovery points for the VM each day. While the RPO is set to 2 hours and if the number of point-in-time instances is set to 4, then you have only 4 snapshots for that VM. VR tries to keep the oldest of the recovery points created.

Once a replication has been successfully configured, the destination datastore is populated with the following files:

- `*.vmdk`: This is the base disk(s) to which the VM data is being replicated to

- `hbrdisk.RDID-*`: This is the redo logfile that has the latest replication data

- `hbrcfg*.vmx`: This is a shadow VMX file that will be used to register the VM when a recovery is initiated

The following screenshot shows the contents of the replica VM's directory:

```
/vmfs/volumes/51a9404b-4743f043-59b4-000c29100f1c/XP VM # ls -ltrh
-rw-------    1 root     root          492 Jun 12 06:19 XP VM.vmdk
-rw-------    1 root     root          492 Jun 12 06:19 XP VM_1.vmdk
-rw-------    1 root     root         2.0G Jun 12 06:21 XP VM_1-flat.vmdk
-rw-------    1 root     root         2.9K Jun 12 06:29 hbrcfg.GID-9138c2e5-a6b6-4a6a-aa15-54dc6c9921f4.38.vmxf.113
-rw-------    1 root     root         4.7K Jun 12 06:29 hbrcfg.GID-9138c2e5-a6b6-4a6a-aa15-54dc6c9921f4.38.vmx.112
-rw-------    1 root     root          369 Jun 12 06:29 hbrdisk.RDID-5a727416-7067-4476-b858-645b532bd1db.91.19959393
-rw-------    1 root     root         8.0K Jun 12 06:29 hbrdisk.RDID-5a727416-7067-4476-b858-645b532bd1db.91.19959393
-rw-------    1 root     root         8.5K Jun 12 06:29 hbrcfg.GID-9138c2e5-a6b6-4a6a-aa15-54dc6c9921f4.38.nvram.114
-rw-------    1 root     root         4.1K Jun 12 06:29 hbrgrp.GID-9138c2e5-a6b6-4a6a-aa15-54dc6c9921f4.txt
-rw-------    1 root     root          369 Jun 12 06:29 hbrdisk.RDID-609f252b-20a3-4454-841b-6128635eb120.92.26463666
-rw-------    1 root     root        20.0K Jun 12 06:29 hbrdisk.RDID-609f252b-20a3-4454-841b-6128635eb120.92.26463666
-rw-------    1 root     root         8.0G Jun 12 06:29 XP VM-flat.vmdk
/vmfs/volumes/51a9404b-4743f043-59b4-000c29100f1c/XP VM #
```

 If a VM being replicated is modified by adding a new VMDK to it, then the active replication will stop with an error. The replication should then be manually reconfigured by the administrator to include the new VMDK and resume the replication.

Using the replication seeds

When you configure a replication on a virtual machine for the very first time, the vSphere Replication will need to make an initial copy of the virtual machine's VMDKs. The initial copy can be bandwidth-intensive and time-consuming, based on the size of the VMDKs. We can overcome this by transporting the VMDKs to the intended location, prior to configuring the replication on the VM. The transport method can be of your choice, ideally couriered to the destination site, if remote.

The copies of the VMDKs transported and placed at the destination datastore are referred to as seeds.

The following procedure will guide you through the steps required to use an available seed for a VM:

1. Shut down the virtual machine at the source (protected) site, which you intend to replicate.

2. Copy the virtual machine's folder to the target datastore. If it is in a different datacenter, then the files need to be transported to the datacenter first and then uploaded to the target datastore.

3. Power on the virtual machine at the source (protected) site.

4. Right-click on the virtual machine from the inventory and navigate to the **Configure Replication** tab in **All vSphere Replication Actions**.

5. Select the intended target site and click on **Next**.

6. You will now have an option to manually select a VR Server to pass the replication traffic through or to let VRMS do the selection. Make an intended selection and click on **Next**.

7. Select a datastore where you would like to place the replica of the virtual machine, and set the **Target location** as the folder corresponding to the copy of the source VM at the destination datastore. To do this, hit the **Browse** button to bring up the **Select Target Location** window, as shown in the following screenshot:

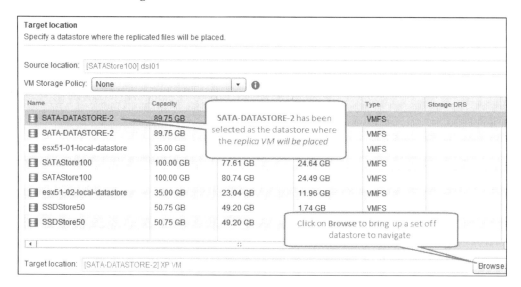

8. The **Select Target Location** window will help you browse the selected datastore. Locate and select the seed VM's folder, and then click on **OK** to confirm the selection and return to the replication configuration wizard.

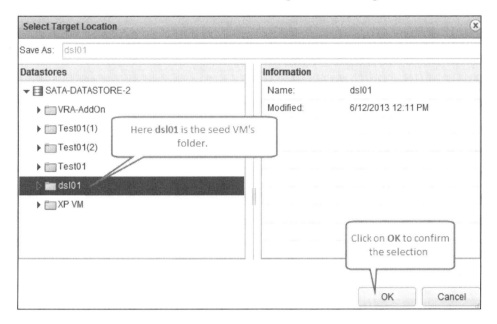

9. Click on **Next** to continue.

10. A **Replication Seed Confirmation** message, revealing that duplicates of the VMDKs were found, will be presented seeking your confirmation to use them as seeds. Click on **Yes** to confirm.

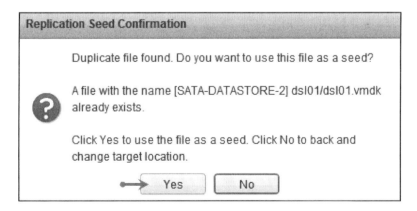

If the VM being replicated has multiple VMDKs and if the duplicate of each VMDK is found, then there will be a **Replication Seed Confirmation** message for each VMDK, as shown in the following screenshot:

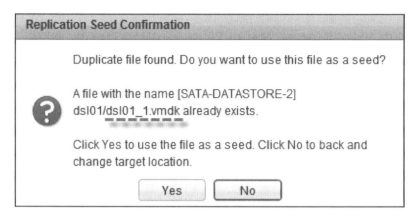

11. Select the virtual disk format and click on **Next** to continue. If the VM being replicated has multiple VMDKs, then there will be a prompt to select the disk format for each VMDK.

12. Choose a guest OS-quiescing method.

13. Set a planned RPO value.

14. You can choose **Enable multiple points in time snapshots** and also specify the number of points you would prefer to be retained. Make the planned selections and click on **Next** to continue.

15. On the **Ready to complete** screen, review the settings and click on **Finish** to configure the replication.

16. The **Recent Tasks** pane should show a **Configure a virtual machine for replication** task as completed successfully.

Regardless of whether you choose to use a seed or not, vSphere Replication always does initiate an initial full sync. With the case of using a seed, the initial full sync will take considerably less time.

Monitoring a replication

Replications configured on virtual machines can be monitored for their current status. Replications can be incoming or outgoing.

The following procedure will guide you through the steps required to monitor a replication:

1. Connect to the vCenter Server and navigate to the inventory home.

2. Click on **vSphere Replication** to bring up the vSphere Replication home page.

3. Click on **Monitor** to go to the monitor tab with the **vSphere Replication** subtab selected.

4. In the left pane, you will find both **Outgoing Replications** and **Incoming Replications** selected.

 The **Outgoing Replications** section will show all the replications leaving the VR Server at the current site, and the **Incoming Replications** section will show all the replications arriving at the VR at the current site.

5. Selecting either **Incoming Replications** or **Outgoing Replications** will list the names of the VMs being replicated and the current status of the replication.

6. At the **Monitor** tab, you will get options to reconfigure, pause, synchronize, stop, and move an ongoing replication. More information on these tasks has been covered in separate sections of this chapter.

Reconfiguring a replication

An ongoing replication can be reconfigured. This is done when there is a need to change the replication server in use, the target datastore, or the recovery settings.

The following procedure will guide you through the steps required to reconfigure a replication:

1. Connect to the vCenter Server and navigate to the inventory home.

2. Click on **vSphere Replication** to bring up the vSphere Replication home page.

3. Click on **Monitor** to go to the monitor tab with the **vSphere Replication** subtab selected.

4. In the left pane, you will find both **Outgoing Replications** and **Incoming Replications** selected. Make an appropriate selection depending on whether you are at the local or the remote vCenter Server.

5. Select the intended replication and click on the **Reconfigure** option in the **Actions** menu to start the reconfiguration wizard, as shown in the following screenshot:

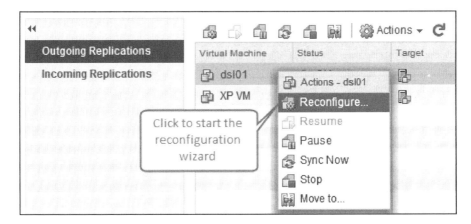

6. Change the replication server to handle the traffic, if intended. Click on **Next** to continue.

7. Select the new target datastore, if intended, and click on **Next** to continue.

8. Modify **Replication Options**, if intended, and click on **Next** to continue.

9. Modify **Recovery Settings**, if intended, and click on **Next** to continue.

10. Review the **Ready to complete** screen and click on **Finish** to initiate the reconfiguration.

Changing the target datastore

You can change the target datastore of an ongoing replication by reconfiguring the replication. Doing so will result in the deletion of the files from the current destination datastore, and an initial full sync will be performed again to the new target datastore location.

The following procedure will guide you through the steps required to change the target datastore of an ongoing replication:

1. Connect to the vCenter Server and navigate to the inventory home page.

2. Click on **vSphere Replication** to bring up the vSphere Replication home page.

3. Click on **Monitor** to go to the monitor tab with the **vSphere Replication** subtab selected.

4. In the left pane, you will find both **Outgoing Replications** and **Incoming Replications** as selected. Make an appropriate selection depending on whether you are at the local or the remote vCenter Server.

5. Select the replication and click on the **Reconfigure** option in the **Actions** menu to start the reconfiguration wizard.

6. Select a replication server to handle the traffic. In this case, we have selected the local VRA. Click on **Next** to continue.

7. Select the new target datastore. As shown in the following screenshot, the **Target location validation** window will appear and show a warning indicating that the existing replicas will be lost. Click on **Next** to continue.

Target location validation:

 Changing the target location requires vSphere Replication to unconfigure and then reconfigure the replication. All replication instances will be lost, and an initial full sync to the new location will be performed. Click the help button for more details.

 There will be multiple prompts to select the target datastore if the VM has multiple VMDKs.

8. Do not modify **Replication Options,** and click on **Next** to continue.

9. Do not modify **Recovery Settings,** and click on **Next** to continue.

10. Review the **Ready to complete** screen and click on **Finish** to initiate the reconfiguration.

11. You should see a **Reconfigure virtual machine replication** task as completed successfully in the **Recent Tasks** pane.

12. The status should read **Initial Full Sync**. If the initial full sync to the new location completes successfully, the status will then read **OK**.

Pausing an ongoing replication

An ongoing replication can be paused regardless of the status it is in. Pausing a replication will stop VR from tracking the changes to the VMDK files. The following procedure will guide you through the steps required to pause an ongoing replication:

1. Connect to the vCenter Server and navigate to the inventory home page.

2. Click on **vSphere Replication** to bring up the vSphere Replication home page.

3. Click on **Monitor** to go to the monitor tab with the **vSphere Replication** subtab selected.

4. In the left pane, you will find both **Outgoing Replications** and **Incoming Replications** as selected. Make an appropriate selection depending on whether you are at the local or the remote vCenter Server.

5. Select the replication that you want to pause and click on the **Pause** option in the **Actions** menu, as shown in the following screenshot:

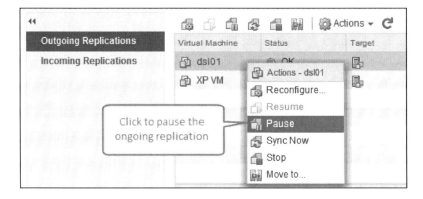

6. Click on **Yes** on the confirmation window.

7. Once the replication has been successfully stopped, the status should read **Paused**.

On pausing an ongoing replication, the VR Server will temporarily stop monitoring the source VM. A paused replication can then be resumed by following the same procedure, but select the **Resume** option in the **Actions** menu as a fifth step.

Synchronizing data immediately

Synchronization is the process of transferring changed blocks from the source to the replica at the destination via the vSphere Replication Server component. vSphere Replication synchronizes the data based on the RPO setting. If the RPO is set to 4 hours, then the synchronization happens every 4 hours.

However, we do have an option to force an immediate synchronization, by using the **Synchronize Data Immediately** option available as a toolbar icon in the **Monitor** tab or the **Sync Now** option available via the action menu. Both options initiate the same task.

The following procedure will guide you through the steps required to initiate the immediate data synchronization:

1. Connect to the vCenter Server and navigate to the inventory home.

2. Click on **vSphere Replication** to bring up the vSphere Replication home page.

3. Click on **Monitor** to go to the monitor tab with the **vSphere Replication** subtab selected.

4. In the left pane, you will find both **Outgoing Replications** and **Incoming Replications** as selected. Make an appropriate selection depending on whether you are at the local or the remote vCenter Server.

5. Select the replication that you want to pause and click on the **Sync Now** tab in the **Actions** menu, as shown in the following screenshot:

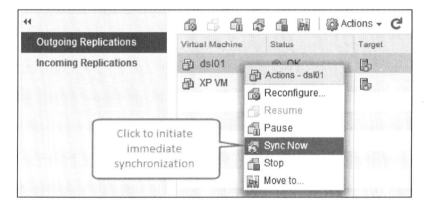

6. You should see a **Synchronize virtual machine** task complete successfully in the **Recent Tasks** pane.

Stopping a replication on a VM

You can choose to stop the replication on a VM if there is a need to do so. Stopping a replication will permanently stop it and delete all the replicas. This is normally done to remove the replication for a VM.

The following procedure will guide you through the steps required to stop replication of a virtual machine:

1. Connect to the vCenter Server and navigate to the inventory home page.

2. Click on **vSphere Replication** to bring up the vSphere Replication home page.

3. Click on **Monitor** to go to the monitor tab with the **vSphere Replication** subtab selected.

4. Select **Outgoing Replications** if the VM is at the protected site, **Incoming Replications** if it is at the recovery site, and either of those if it is replicated to the same site as the source.

5. Select the replication, right-click on it, and click on the **Stop** menu item, as shown in the following screenshot:

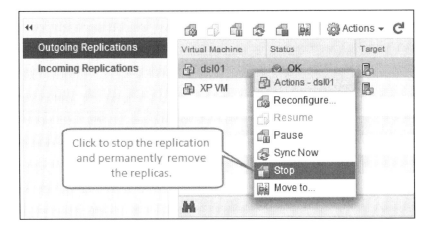

6. You will be prompted to confirm the selection. Click on **Yes** to confirm. Refer to the following screenshot:

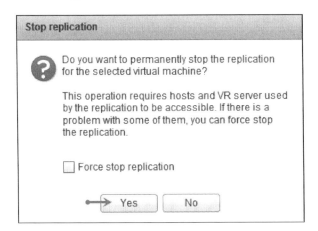

7. The **Recent Tasks** pane should show the two tasks, **Disable Replication of the virtual machine** and **Unconfigure virtual machine replication**, as completed successfully.

8. The **Outgoing Replications** or **Incoming Replications** sections will no longer list the stopped replication.

Moving a replication to another VR Server

You can choose to move an active replication to another vSphere Replication Server if there is a need. This is generally done if you have multiple VR Servers at the recovery site and you intend to distribute the replication load onto those servers. Moving a replication to another VR Server requires a reconfiguring of the replication on the VM.

The following procedure will guide you through the steps required to move the replication to another VR Server:

1. Connect to the vCenter Server and navigate to the inventory home page.

2. Click on **vSphere Replication** to bring up the vSphere Replication home page.

3. Click on **Monitor** to go to the monitor tab with the **vSphere Replication** subtab selected.

4. Select either **Outgoing Replications** or **Incoming Replications**.

5. Select the replication, right-click on it, and click on the **Move to** menu item, as shown in the following screenshot:

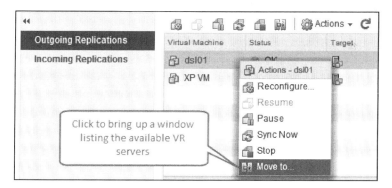

6. You should now be presented with a list of vSphere Replication Servers registered to the site the VM is being replicated to. Make a selection and click on **OK**. Refer to the following screenshot:

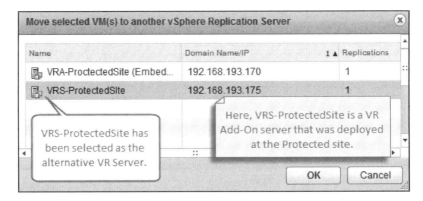

7. The **Recent Tasks** pane should show the **Move replication to other VR Server** task as completed successfully and the status should read **OK**.

Recovering virtual machines

Now that we have described how to configure replication for the virtual machines, the story will remain half told if we do not cover how to recover virtual machines using their replicas. You perform a recovery only at the target site. In other words, you will be presented with an option to initiate a recovery only at the site that has seen the incoming replication.

The following procedure will guide you through the steps required to perform a recovery:

1. Connect to the vCenter Server managing the remote site and navigate to the inventory home page.

If there is only one vCenter Server managing both the protected and recovery sites, then vSphere Replication's **Monitor** tab will show both the outgoing and incoming replications for the virtual machine.

2. Click on **vSphere Replication** to bring up the vSphere Replication home page.

3. Click on **Monitor** to go to the monitor tab with the **vSphere Replication** subtab selected.

4. Select **Incoming Replications** from the left pane and select the virtual machine you would like to recover.

5. With the virtual machine selected, right-click on it and click on **Recover**.

6. You will be presented with the recovery options: **Recover with recent changes** and **Recover with the latest available data**. Choose an intended option and click on **Next** to continue. More insight on these options will be included at the end of this section. Refer to the following screenshot:

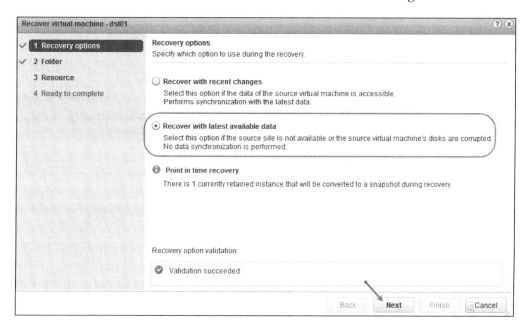

7. Select the datacenter/folder you intend to place the VM in. Only the datacenter to which the virtual machine was replicated can be selected. Refer to the following screenshot:

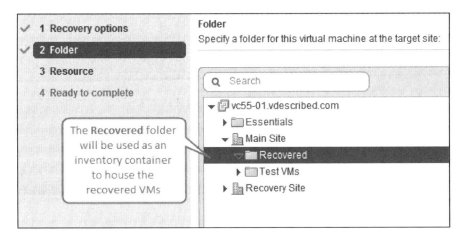

 You will not be able to place the recovered VM into the same inventory-hierarchical level as that of the source VM. It is a general practice to create a folder under the datacenter level to house the recovered VMs.

8. Click on **Next** to continue.

9. Select the compute resource (cluster/host/resource pool) and click on **Next**.

10. If you still have leftover files at the source datastore, then you will be prompted to overwrite. Click on **Yes** to confirm.

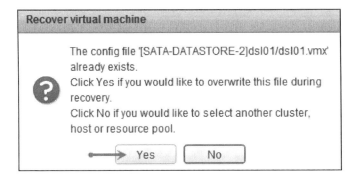

11. Click on **Next** to continue.

12. On the **Ready to complete** screen, you can choose not to power on the recovered virtual machine by deselecting the **Power on the virtual machine after recovery** checkbox. It is selected (checked) by default. Click on **Finish** to start the recovery.

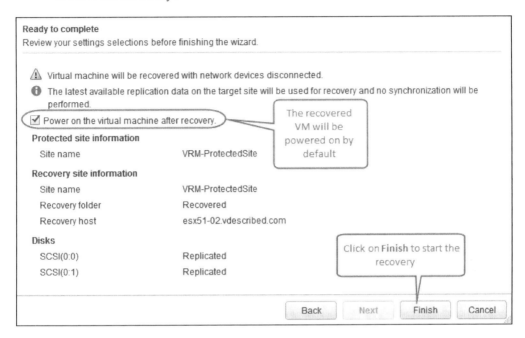

13. The **Recent Tasks** pane should show a **Recover Virtual Machine** task as completed successfully. The replication status of the VM will show as **Recovered**.

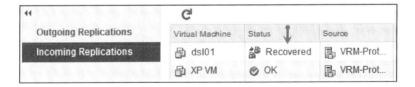

After a successful recovery, the inventory should show the recovered VM listed and powered on.

Recover with recent changes

This option will initiate an immediate synchronization to make sure that the VM after recovery has the latest data in it. This is, however, not possible if the source VM is powered on. You will have to manually power off the VM if it is running.

Recover with the latest available data

This option will recover using the most recent redo log that was created. In this case, you will lose all the changes that happened at the source VM since the last replication. The amount of data loss will not exceed the RPO set. For instance, if the RPO was set to 15 minutes, then you would only lose 15 minutes worth of data.

Configuring a Failback for virtual machines

With vSphere Replication, configuring a Failback for a virtual machine is a manual process. The following process will guide you through the steps required to perform a Failback:

1. Recover the virtual machine to the recovery site. Read the *Recovering virtual machines* section for instructions.

2. Remove the virtual machine from the inventory on the protected site.

3. Configure an outgoing replication from the recovery site to the protected site. Read the *Configuring a replication of a VM to a remote site* section for instructions.

When configuring the replication from the recovery to the protected site, if the datastore at the protected site has the VM files, then those can be used as seeds; otherwise, an initial full sync is performed.

 A Failover can be automated using Site Recovery Manager.

Configuring SRM to leverage vSphere Replication

vSphere Replication as a standalone product has no ability to automate DR tasks, such as a test, a Failover, or a Failback. SRM can be used to leverage vSphere Replication as the replication engine and use its orchestration ability to automate the DR tasks. Refer to the following diagram:

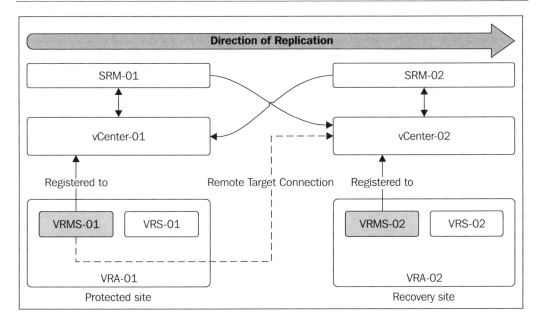

SRM relies on the concept of two sites that replicates data between them with the help of a replication engine. So, you need two sites managed separately by two different vCenter Servers. Both the vCenter Servers should have a VRMS instance registered to it. Meaning, you need to deploy a **vSphere Replication Appliance (VRA)** at both the sites. Once the VRA is deployed, use the vSphere Web Client's vSphere Replication interface at the protected site to add the recovery site as the target site. For more information on how to add target sites, read the *Adding a remote site as a target* section. Now, for SRM to detect the registered vSphere Replication Appliances at both the sites, you will need to install the vSphere Replication component bundled with the SRM installer. If you already have SRM installed, you can run the installer to repair the installer and install vSphere Replication components as well. Once you have installed the vSphere Replication component, the SRM interface should list vSphere Replication.

All the DR tasks that can be performed using SRM have been explained in the chapters that cover SRM's array-based replication. Although the DR tasks are notably similar, there are a few changes to the workflow.

We will cover the following tasks in this section:

- Creating a vSphere Replication Protection Group
- Creating a vSphere Replication Recovery Plan
- Testing a vSphere Replication Recovery Plan
- Performing a Failover (Recovery)
- Performing a Failback (reprotect and Failover)

Creating a vSphere Replication Protection Group

You will need to create a Protection Group for the virtual machines you would like to protect using vSphere Replication. Unlike the array-based replication, you can select any replication-enabled virtual machine to become a part of a Protection Group.

To do this, perform the following steps:

1. Navigate to the vCenter Server's inventory home page and click on **Site Recovery**.
2. Click on **Protection Groups** on the left pane.
3. Click on **Create Protection Group** to bring up the **Create Protection Group** wizard.
4. In the wizard, select the **Protection Group Type** as **vSphere Replication (VR)** and click on **Next** to continue.
5. The next screen will provide you with a list of all the replication-enabled virtual machines. Choose the ones you want to include in the Protection Group and click on **Next** to continue.
6. Provide a name and an optional description for the Protection Group and click on **Next** to continue.
7. On the **Ready to Complete** screen, click on **Finish** to create the Protection Group.

You should now see the **Create Protection Group** and **Protect VM** task as completed successfully in the **Recent Tasks** pane. At the **Recovery Site**, you should see a **Shadow Virtual Machine** created for the virtual machines we added to the Protection Group.

Creating a vSphere Replication Recovery Plan

Once the Protection Groups are created, the next step is to create Recovery Plans.

To do this, perform the following steps:

1. Navigate to the vCenter Server's inventory home page and click on **Site Recovery**.

2. Click on **Recovery Plans** in the left pane and click on **Create Recovery Plan** to bring up the **Create Recovery Plan** wizard.

3. The remote site is chosen as the recovery site by default. Click on **Next** to continue.

4. Select a Protection Group of the type VR. Note that this window will also display Protection Groups of the array-based type, if there are any. So, make sure that you select a Protection Group of the type VR and click on **Next** to continue.

5. Choose **Recovery Network** and **Test Network**. You can leave the **Test Network** at **Auto** if you intend to use the temporary vSwitch and the port group that SRM creates for the test; otherwise, you could choose another port group that you have created for the testing. Click on **Next** to continue.

6. Provide a **Recovery Plan Name** and an optional description and then click on **Next** to continue.

7. In the **Ready to Complete** screen, review the options and click on **Finish** to create the Recovery Plan.

You should see a **Create Recovery Plan** task as completed successfully in the **Recent Tasks** pane.

Testing a vSphere Replication Recovery Plan

Any Recovery Plan that you create should be periodically tested to make sure that it is ready for a DR activity, should the need arise.

This is done by performing the following steps:

1. Navigate to the vCenter Server's inventory home page and click on **Site Recovery**.

2. Click on **Recovery Plans** in the left pane and choose a plan for a vSphere Replication Protection Group.

3. Click on the **Test** button to bring up the **Test wizard**.

4. By default, the **Replicate recent changes to recovery site** checkbox is selected. Leave it selected and click on **Next** to continue.

5. On the next screen, review the options and click on **Start** to begin the test operation.

The progress of the recovery steps can be monitored in the **Recovery Steps** tab.

Make sure that you run a cleanup after the test is complete.

Performing a Recovery or a Planned Migration

In the event of a disaster at the protected site or when there is the need for a Planned Migration, we can use SRM's Recovery option to run the Recovery Plan to perform either of the tasks. A Planned Migration and a Recovery are different in terms of whether the replication of the recent changes is necessary. A Planned Migration cannot proceed without being able to replicate the recent changes. A disaster recovery will attempt to replicate the recent changes, but it would continue even if it is unable to do so.

The procedure is the same regardless of the replication engine in use. Refer to the *Performing a Planned Migration* and *Performing a disaster recovery (Failover)* sections from *Chapter 3, Testing and Performing a Failover and Failback*.

A Recovery is always from the recovery site. Once initiated, a new sync is initiated to replicate the recent changes. Once done, the protected virtual machine is powered off, and the replication status is changed to recovered.

Performing a Failback (reprotect and Failover)

After a Failover, you can enable protection of the virtual machines in the reverse order, which is achieved by running a reprotect operation. Refer to the following diagram:

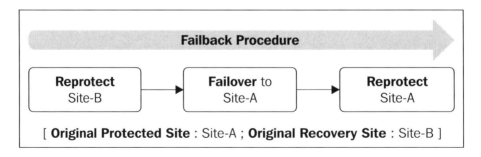

A reprotect will reverse the direction of the replication. Now, after the original protected site becomes operational, you could choose to Failback to the original site. This is achieved by issuing a Failover after a successful reprotect operation. Once the Failover is complete, the replication status would be set to recovered, and there will not be an active replication. To re-enable a replication in the original direction, you should run a reprotect operation again.

Summary

In the previous chapter, you learned how to set up a vSphere Replication environment, and then use it to configure a replication on virtual machines. We also learned how to stop or pause an ongoing replication and how to move the replication load onto another vSphere Replication Server. More importantly, we learned how to recover a virtual machine from a replica. Most of the replication-related activities that we have discussed in the chapter are done on a per VM basis, and that is all you can do with vSphere Replication when implemented as a standalone solution. We then learned how to configure vCenter Site Recovery Manager to leverage the vSphere Replication and perform the disaster recovery tasks.

Index

Thank you for buying
Disaster Recovery Using VMware vSphere Replication and vCenter Site Recovery Manager

About Packt Publishing

Packt, pronounced 'packed', published its first book "Mastering phpMyAdmin for Effective MySQL Management" in April 2004 and subsequently continued to specialize in publishing highly focused books on specific technologies and solutions.

Our books and publications share the experiences of your fellow IT professionals in adapting and customizing today's systems, applications, and frameworks. Our solution based books give you the knowledge and power to customize the software and technologies you're using to get the job done. Packt books are more specific and less general than the IT books you have seen in the past. Our unique business model allows us to bring you more focused information, giving you more of what you need to know, and less of what you don't.

Packt is a modern, yet unique publishing company, which focuses on producing quality, cutting-edge books for communities of developers, administrators, and newbies alike. For more information, please visit our website: www.packtpub.com.

About Packt Enterprise

In 2010, Packt launched two new brands, Packt Enterprise and Packt Open Source, in order to continue its focus on specialization. This book is part of the Packt Enterprise brand, home to books published on enterprise software – software created by major vendors, including (but not limited to) IBM, Microsoft and Oracle, often for use in other corporations. Its titles will offer information relevant to a range of users of this software, including administrators, developers, architects, and end users.

Writing for Packt

We welcome all inquiries from people who are interested in authoring. Book proposals should be sent to author@packtpub.com. If your book idea is still at an early stage and you would like to discuss it first before writing a formal book proposal, contact us; one of our commissioning editors will get in touch with you.

We're not just looking for published authors; if you have strong technical skills but no writing experience, our experienced editors can help you develop a writing career, or simply get some additional reward for your expertise.

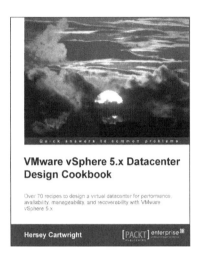

VMware vSphere 5.x Datacenter Design Cookbook

ISBN: 978-1-78217-700-5   Paperback: 260 pages

Over 70 recipes to design a virtual datacenter for performance, availability, manageability, and recoverability with VMware vSphere 5.x

1. Innovative recipes, offering numerous practical solutions when designing virtualized datacenters.

2. Identify the design factors—requirements, assumptions, constraints, and risks—by conducting stakeholder interviews and performing technical assessments.

VMware Workstation – No Experience Necessary

ISBN: 978-1-84968-918-2   Paperback: 136 pages

Get started with VMware Workstation to create virtual machines and a virtual testing platform

1. Create virtual machines on Linux and Windows hosts.

2. Create advanced test labs that help in getting back to any Virtual Machine state in an easy way.

3. Share virtual machines with others, no matter which virtualization solution they're using.

Please check **www.PacktPub.com** for information on our titles

Implementing VMware vCenter Server

ISBN: 978-1-84968-998-4   Paperback: 324 pages

A practical guide for deploying and using VMware vCenter, suitable for IT professionals

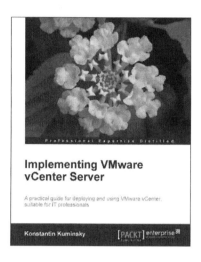

1. Gain in-depth knowledge of the VMware vCenter features, requirements, and deployment process.

2. Manage hosts, virtual machines, and learn storage management in VMware vCenter server.

3. Overview of VMware vCenter Operations Manager and VMware vCenter Orchestrator.

VMware vSphere 5.1 Cookbook

ISBN: 978-1-84968-402-6   Paperback: 466 pages

Over 130 task-oriented recipes to install, configure, and manage various vSphere 5.1 components

1. Install and configure vSphere 5.1 core components.

2. Learn important aspects of vSphere such as administration, security, and performance.

3. Configure vSphere Management Assistant (VMA) to run commands/scripts without the need to authenticate every attempt.

Please check **www.PacktPub.com** for information on our titles

Made in the USA
Middletown, DE
24 March 2015